JUSTICE DENIED

A Brief Disquisition and Diatribe Against Bail/ Bonding, Plea Bargaining, Probation, and Parole with Ancillary Remarks on Crimes Without Victims, Recreational Drug Laws, Blue Laws, Gun Legislation, and Incarceration

ROBERT HAUPTMAN

ANAPHORA LITERARY PRESS

QUANAH, TEXAS

Anaphora Literary Press
1108 W 3rd Street
Quanah, TX 79252
https://anaphoraliterary.com

Book design by Anna Faktorovich, Ph.D.

Printed in the United States of America, United Kingdom and in Australia on acid-free paper.

Cover Images: Cover Art: Honoré Victorin Daumier, "I really gave you a good dressing down", 1845, Print Sales Miscellaneous Fund: Art Institute Chicago.
Guillaume Dupré, "Justice with Sword and Scales", 1623. Samuel H. Kress Collection: National Gallery of Art.
Angeline Starr, "Gavel", c. 1940, Index of American Design: National Gallery of Art.

Published in 2025 by Anaphora Literary Press

Justice Denied
Robert Hauptman—1st edition.

Library of Congress Control Number: 2025908603

Library Cataloging Information

Hauptman, Robert, 1941-, author.
Justice denied : A brief disquisition and diatribe against bail/bonding, plea bargaining, probation, and parole with ancillary remarks on crimes without victims, recreational drug laws, blue laws, gun legislation, and incarceration / Robert Hauptman
134 p. ; 9 in.
ISBN 978-1-68114-623-2 (softcover : alk. paper)
ISBN 978-1-68114-624-9 (hardcover : alk. paper)
Kindle (e-book)
1. Books—Law—Criminal Law—Criminal Procedure.
2. Books—Law—Legal Theory & Systems—Judicial System.
3. Books—Law—Ethics & Professional Responsibility.
K5401-5570: Criminal Procedure
345: Criminal Law

CONTENTS

A true vision of moral justice cannot readily
be integrated into the legal establishment.
—Thane Rosenbaum

Foreword

The American legal system, including the criminal justice system and the body of law that has accumulated over the years are all works in progress. Beginning in the aftermath of the American Revolution when the work of drafting a constitution was complete, judges and other key administrators in the fledgling country were faced with the question of where to turn for a source of law while observing the blank slate they were just handed. Repugnant as it was, many of the new states turned back to the English Common Law for the first few decades until a truly domestic body of jurisprudence could be developed. The states eventually went off on their own in a spirit of independence, with courts handing down opinions and legislatures passing statutes without much concern for what their neighbors were doing. As time went by, statutory law grew in importance and largely usurped the Common Law in many legal subject areas, the largest exceptions being tort and property law. Today to the casual observer, especially in our political climate, the legislative part of the process seems particularly static, interrupted occasionally by small changes to the law here and there. It's largely a reactive system with major developments mostly occurring after catastrophes or significant social change. In the Sixties the Civil Rights movement led to several legislative actions affecting employment, housing, and voting among others. The Seventies saw the start of the environmental movement with accompanying legislation. The work of the judiciary is by nature backwards looking also, dealing with actions that have for the most part already occurred. Over two hundred years after the Revolution this is the situation in which we find ourselves. Fifty-one jurisdictions perpetuating often radically different bodies of law, with new enactments sometimes years after the event that cried out for reform. To try and rectify this picture there have been attempts at unification of state law through things like model and uniform statutes, mostly on the civil side, drafted by organizations and commissions, with a few successes and many near misses. This tale wouldn't be complete without mentioning the role of finance in the mix. The federal and state capitals are full of lobbyists trying to influence the work that is done there. It can be just as interesting to see which bills don't get enacted as those that do. Lobbying has become an industry in itself. The criminal justice system is also influenced by money. It is very clear that those who have the resources will get the best attorneys, researchers, and experts. The number of death row inmates later found innocent after a thorough investigative review speaks to this. The cost of trying and housing those accused of or convicted of a crime can also be a factor in some policy decisions.

This is the situation that Robert Hauptman has taken aim at. He has chosen several legal areas to investigate, things that are long due for an overhaul or processes that are biased or illogical. The absurdity of our minimalist gun laws is an example. As school children are butchered repeatedly in classrooms and hallways our courts and legislators turn a blind eye to the situation by citation to an ancient provision in the Constitution originally drafted for reasons that no longer exist. It is this kind of nonsense that Hauptman rails against. After discussing the pros and cons of a law or procedure, he sets out the basis for his thoughts and then provides the major opposing ideas along with details of some of the reforms different jurisdictions (both domestic and foreign have put in place. A review of relevant literature and major court cases are also part of each package. This is all interesting and helpful but it's not enough. Hauptman is not willing to stop with just a review of the law, he's interested in the moral situation that arises from each of these problem areas. Law and ethics are not always on the same track with each other, sometimes veering wildly apart. Whether he is talking about a criminal or a victim there is a moral underpinning to everything he writes.

Some of the subjects Hauptman delves into are a bit sensitive and some have been debated for decades if not centuries without a consensus. In a few cases he makes it clear that he knows it is unlikely that the issues will be resolved in the near future. Not every reader is going to agree with all the ideas presented in this book or with the topics singled out for reform. Hauptman is not trying to change the world, just a little piece of it. He gives us much to think about and enough to keep the dialog going.

Marc Silverman
Director (retired) Barco Law Library
University of Pittsburgh

Acronyms

ACLU American Civil Liberties Union
ALS Amyotrophic lateral sclerosis (Lou Gehrig's disease)
AMA American Medical Association
ATF Bureau of Alcohol, Tobacco and Firearms
AWOL Away without leave
BLM Black Lives Matter
C LS Critical Legal Studies
CRT Critical Race Theory
DEI Diversity, Equity, Inclusion
EU European Union
JAMA *Journal of the American Medical Association*
MS Multiple sclerosis
NIH National Institutes of Health
NRA National Rifle Association
PAC Political Action Committee
UK United Kingdom
US United States of America
WHO Would Health Organization

Preface

The following concise monograph, *Justice Denied: A Brief Disquisition and Diatribe Against Bail/Bonding, Plea Bargaining, Probation, and Parole with Ancillary Remarks on Crimes Without Victims, Recreational Drug Laws, Blue Laws, Gun Legislation, and Incarceration,* is a critique of a number of allegedly beneficial processes, procedures, and legal protocols that are in reality quite harmful. An extremely high percentage of laypersons, scholars, organizations, lawyers, and jurists agree that they are problematic and should be reformed or abolished. Surprisingly, though, a few thinkers disagree. An excellent example is George Fisher, who instead of decrying plea bargaining, tells us that it is triumphant, which is really perverse.

Four issues—assisted suicide and gender transition but especially abortion and gun legislation—are extremely controversial. More than three quarters of Americans favor abortion while not quite as many desire stricter gun laws. The precise statistics in both cases are elusive, since different polls result in varying percentages.

And this brings to the fore statistical citations. They vary because the statisticians, analysts, pollsters, polls, locations, and other factors influence the results which can vary and clash. In my *Desert Encyclopedia,* which Lyons Press published in August of 2024, the areas of deserts are sometimes so indeterminate that I include various numbers as in the case of the Great Basin Desert which is 150,000, 175,000 to 208,000 square miles. Quite a range, no? Be wary of statistics: they may confuse, distort, mislead, or lie.

Introduction

Justice Denied is a succinct, iconoclastic analysis and condemnation of a number of legal processes that appear at first sight to be beneficial but which in reality are primarily harmful and often allow those guilty of heinous crimes to go at least partially unpunished, and further hamper attempts to protect society. Of the four types of justice—distributive (who gets what), procedural (how fairly people are treated), retributive (punishment), and restorative (restores matters)—I am here concerned with retribution. And this is because I am primarily interested in egregious breaches of social interaction such as embezzlements, Ponzi schemes, and extreme cybercrime that financially harm millions of people; assault, mugging, and car jacking that physically injure; and premeditated murder of strangers, friends, spouses, lovers, or parents, a crime so heinous that it must remain unforgiven except by the angelically liberal. The theorists preach restoration but if it were their family that had been slaughtered, they might have a different take on the jury's acquittal. As for those guilty of lesser crimes such as minor thefts, vandalism, decorating walls and subway cars with graffiti, and so on, they should not be incarcerated at all. They should be required to work, earn money, and repay their victims. In the US, we care more about property crime than physical harm to people. Teenagers who break a store window will receive a harsher punishment than those who bully their peers.

I am not alone in calling for fairness, justice, and punishment. Thane Rosenbaum's *Payback* is a nuanced argument in favor of taking an eye for an eye, a tooth for a tooth, if not literally, which would constitute cruel and unusual (biblical) punishment, but metaphorically, so that the punishment fits the crime. Sadly, I am not interested in restoring to society the rapists and killers who went astray and now are such upstanding if incarcerated citizens. Sirhan Sirhan, who murdered Bobby Kennedy, has come up for parole 15 times; he really wants to return to society a free man. He should have thought about his future—which would have ended in death had California not outlawed the death penalty—before assassinating an innocent man, one who served his country in many capacities. Sirhan exemplifies the criminal who deserves very little consideration or sympathy, one who should have to serve out his sentence. When a judge sentences a Nathan Leopold, who committed a most barbaric crime, to life plus 99 years, he should not be paroled 34 years later, as he was. He went on to a pleasant existence in Puerto Rico. His pathological collaborator Richard Loeb was murdered in prison. By the way, it is interesting to note that these two sociopaths suffered from a bizarre "syndrome" (not those that Clarence Darrow cited at the trial), one that I describe as being too smart for one's own good: Loeb's IQ was 160 and Leopold registered more than 210. (There was a time when John Stuart Mill at 210 [now 180-190] was postulated to have had the highest IQ, but now the testers speak of 300 and even 400, which seems impossible. At 400, one's brain might very well implode.)

Much that follows deals with superfluous, misleading, or harmful legislation. But surprisingly, there exist some crucial areas in which the laws against certain actions are outdated, inadequate, or far too lenient. Examples include financial fraud, identity theft, and especially cybercrime through which sometimes foreign actors wreak havoc with computer systems or demand ransoms. Shutting down a hospital's systems can result in patients' physical harm or even death. Though liberal criminologists will disagree, insisting that harsh penalties have little effect on the crime rate, extraditing a Russian hacker and locking him up for 100 years will rid the world of at least one parasite. Well, perhaps 100 years is too long. How about 50?

The law's evolution, foibles, harm, and injustice have long been of interest to popular story tellers, but especially classical novelists, among whom are Dickens (lengthy court case bankrupts everyone), Hugo (sentenced to five years for stealing a loaf of bread), Dostoevsky (justice not served), Kafka (on trial for no apparent reason), Camus (sentenced for a social taboo), and Harper Lee (protecting innocence).

The Law and Its Precedents

The law is a very tricky business. Even small, primitive social groups have taboos, customs, rules, and "laws" that control members' actions. Contravening these may have devastating consequences, but not always: Recall how males in Margaret Mead's Samoa snuck around for sexual interaction even though this was forbidden. In large societies, with many millions of constituents, a complex and diversified controlling legal system is necessary because when many humans gather, there are bound to be thugs and hoodlums, thieves and murderers among them. The law in historical times has derived from monarchical fiat or elected bodies such as parliaments, state legislatures, or Congress introducing possibilities, passing them, and having the King or Queen, governor general, governor, or president affirm them. These statutory laws are often but not always reasonable and control social activity. When a law favors slavery or disfavors miscegenation or is unusually cruel or foolish, it can be ignored (to one's peril) or revoked. If this were all there is to legal stricture, it would be quite adequate but there is more.

In the US, when a court case is decided, it may have no bearing whatsoever on future proceedings. This would be so, for example, in traffic court where thoughtless people, who manage to travel 50 miles an hour in a 20 mile an hour school zone, are admonished by the judge, fined $300, and required to do community service, and go on their way. The subsequent hundred proceedings are similar and no one pays much attention as they unroll day after day. But more important cases are carefully scrutinized, recorded, and cited some time thereafter as a similar case unfolds. Since the judge (and jury) decided that a minor caught harassing a middle school teacher cannot be tried as an adult, the defense in the next proceeding cites this case to *prove* that his protege cannot be so tried. The former case has set a precedent (stare decisis) and becomes case law, and it is as difficult to gainsay this type of "legislation" as it would have been in 1967 to successfully fight against the federal law that mandated that one could be drafted in wartime (now defunct) or against the second Amendment. But though useful at times, precedent can also be extremely harmful, affording unjust decisions from the past in order to forward similar outcomes in the present. Imagine a madman citing "repugnant" Korematsu v. US or Buck v. Bell (both of which have never been overturned by the Supreme Court) as precedents!

Precedent forms one of the primary bases of US law and it is rather heretical to criticize it, but I am not alone in condemning it for it is conservative, rigid, complex, and may lead one down an unethical path. Gary S. Lawson, a law professor, insists in "The Constitutional Case against Precedent" that it is often unconstitutional, with certain provisos, to cite previous decisions when rendering a judgment: "The prima facie case against horizontal precedent in federal constitutional adjudication is elegantly simple, devastatingly powerful, and strikingly familiar from other contexts" (25). "The Constitution stands at the apex of our legal system as supreme law, hierarchically superior to all other claimed sources of law. An enactment that has the form of a statute, but that violates the Constitution, has no valid legal status" (26). "Suppose now that a court is faced with a conflict between the Constitution on the one hand and a prior judicial decision on the other. Is there any doubt that, under the reasoning of Marbury, the court must choose the Constitution over the prior decision?" (27). "[*T*]*he constitutional case against precedent is precisely coterminous with the constitutional case for judicial review*" (italics in original 31). "If judges are going to continue to employ precedent, there is value in acknowledging that the practice is nothing more than 'a sort of intellectual adverse possession'—and that the territory adversely possessed is nothing less than the Constitution" (33).

Furthermore, scholars from other disciplines also claim that it can result in disastrous judgments. Erin P. Hennes and Layla Dang, psychologists rather than lawyers, approach the problem from a unique perspective: "Yet the intent of precedent—to safeguard equity—may be undermined by nonconscious psychological processes. The behavioral and brain sciences show that decision-making can be contaminated by a human proclivity (endemic among both judges and laypeople) to justify and legitimize extant societal arrangements" (abstract). Thus, citing precedents, rather than leading juries and judges to equitable and judicious decisions, may result in ongoing injustice merely because a case or cases were decided unconstitutionally, unfairly, or prejudicially 25, 50, or 100 years ago.

Justice

Sometimes a term that appears to be clear and comprehensible turns out to be confusing, often having very different meanings in different eras, cultures, and even to siblings. In ancient Egypt, a person had to be virtuous to be admitted to the afterlife: His or her heart was weighed against a feather; this is an extremely demanding form of justice, for few people maintain a truly virtuous existence. For the Biblical Israelites, justice demanded equal payment: an eye for an eye, a tooth for a tooth. For Shakespeare's Shylock, insisting on his pound of flesh seemed to be warranted justice, but even for Shakespeare's peers, when extreme punishment was not unusual, this obviously was untenable, since this is the point of *The Merchant of Venice.* Justice in contemporary America is represented by the image of a blindfolded woman holding a scale: Justice is blind and impartially weighs the evidence. The conclusion is just, but not always and not for everyone: Today, women, minorities, the poor, the downtrodden, illegal immigrants, and the domestically or sexually abused are dissatisfied with the unjust, unfair, inequitable treatment that is meted out to them by society, employers, spouses, the police, and the court system. In more esoteric terms, they fail to achieve just deserts (which usually has a negative connotation).

Some contemporary well-meaning people, insist that torture is warranted as punishment for egregious crimes such as the bombing of the World Trade Center, in which 2,753 innocent folks lost their lives or to ferret out important (life-saving) information. Others (the Constitution, international law, this author) claim that it is never permissible. It constitutes cruel and unusual punishment, something that was common in the past and which is why the Founding Fathers prohibited it; it is degrading; and it is repugnant to so harm a fellow human being, even a teratism such as Pol Pot or Hitler. This does not mean that justice is not served by capital punishment, which may appear to be rather paradoxical. And slavery is an unjust system and that is why the US Civil War was fought but it did not eliminate it in other countries, and today there are still more than 40 million slaves in countries such as India, North Korea, Mauritania, and, sadly, many others.

In contemporary America, the fanatically religious, capitalists, socialists, Marxists, and communists all have very different conceptions of justice, although in no case would anyone condone the Saudi Arabian customs of lashing or amputation for theft. These sometimes well-meaning people have evolved various ideas for adjectively modifying justice and confusing the layman. We now have climate justice; social justice, which demands equal rights; design justice; and even research justice, which wishes to use the scholarly research process to advance social causes, for example, minority rights and social change generally.

As if conceptions of justice were not complex enough, John Rawls complicates matters in his extremely influential 1971 *Theory of Justice,* which emphasizes economic matters to the exclusion of justice allocated for harm, crime, sedition, espionage, and other malfeasances. Rawls is only interested in distributive justice, that is, an equitable and fair distribution of goods and employment opportunities. In passing, one might observe that after more than half a century, during which society has had the opportunity to improve matters, we have failed because the fair (just) distribution of goods and opportunities is no different than it was when Rawls envisioned his study. And sadly, this is so despite all of the unnecessary deaths and movements including BLM, DEI, CLS, CRT, and other radical incursions in a pliable society. Indeed, it is even the case that postmodern nonsense has managed to infiltrate peer-reviewed hard science journals. Critics will object that wages and salaries have increased quite dramatically (not out of concern, but because the pandemic resulted in many unfilled positions). The truth is that the soaring remuneration at many levels is offset by the extraordinary increase in rent, services, food, and house and automobile costs. Consider that in 1971, a Subaru cost $1,699; in 2023 the cost had risen to almost 27,000. In 1967, a brand new house on Long Island sold for $23,000; in 2023, it went for about 800,000. Progress (justice) is, at least to some extent, illusory. (For a detailed overview see *https://en.wikipedia.org/wiki/Justice*).

Additionally, a major impediment to *just* deserts is, as Rosenbaum points out in *The Myth of Moral Justice,* the disparity between the law and morals, i.e., ethical commitment (30), on the part of lawyers, prosecutors, and judges, who follow the course of the law and legal reasoning as well as necessity to the detriment of what is good and right. He additionally laments the loss of truth as the innocent falsely plead guilty and are incarcerated. This, he claims, is immoral (87) and worse, "Moral justice is further undermined by technicalities, loopholes, and procedural irregularities in the law" (114).

There are, naturally, others who care about the true and fair allocation of justice and the Restore Justice Foundation is an excellent example of an organization that works to this end: Restorative rather than retributive justice is its objective and so it advocates for. "...a safer and more compassionate state [Illinois] by replacing the ineffective, extreme sentencing policies of the past with evidence-based laws that allow families and communities to heal" (*https://www.restorejustice.org/*). It promotes less punitive legislation, and so would I, as long as the sentence is just for both perpetrator and victim. Often it is not and some think that a higher order of justice will eventually prevail. Here is how Sherlock Holmes puts it in the "Boscombe Valley Mystery": "...[Y]ou will have to answer for your deed at a higher court than the assizes." This is as improbable as a guilty person returning as a reincarnated dung beetle.

To get to a lower (that is, human rather than celestial) court in order to have a trial, at least in the US, it is necessary to plead not guilty, even though the perpetrator is blatantly culpable and everyone knows it. This is a bizarre necessity and raises ethical (not legal) problems for anyone who cares about the truth, since it entails lying. Just because someone has done something illegal, say, extreme speeding under duress, and desires to attempt to clear himself before a jury of his peers, does not mean that he is wiling to distort the truth by pleading not guilty (which is a legal tactic, but a lie), since he knows that he is at fault *but with extenuating circumstances.* Justice here is not served.

An additional impediment to a fair hearing and thus justice is the extreme dependence, as noted, that American legal practice places on precedent (which is why law review articles are so long; their authors must cite [and explicate] every germane precedent in interminable footnotes). But legislation and court decisions of the past are sometimes not merely wrong; they are vile. So, just because a judge in 1840 ruled that a robber should be hanged for a minor theft does not mean that this should be the case in 2025. Precedent should be decommissioned.

Retribution

...[T]here is no difference between justice and vengeance.
—Thane Rosenbaum

In *Payback*, Rosenbaum argues persuasively for revenge, a term and activity that most sensitive, caring people now abjure. *But* keep in mind that revenge in the 21st century is not the same thing that was envisioned and carried out in the not so distant past, and as one works her way back in history the acts become more horrendous. If interested in this unpleasant subject, see Michel Foucault's *Discipline and Punish* and the section in Frank Abagnale's *Catch Me if You Can* that describes his imprisonment in a French jail just a few years ago. One is hard pressed to believe that the French could treat a human being in this horrific manner. He subsequently spent time in a Swedish prison; it was like living in an Airbnb.

Revenge has always been an integral part of human identity and culture but it has not always been handled in the same way. Naturally, during the course of human history, individuals and both primitive tribal groups as well as sophisticated societies have repaid those who have harmed them by viciously attacking, torturing, raping, and killing. This is precisely what occurred in 2023 in Israel, when Hamas paid the Israelis back for real and imagined harms by acting in a barbaric manner and murdering 1400 innocent people and taking hostages. Israel, in turn, did the same thing by invading Gaza and harming innocent Gazans, while ironically allowing many Hamas members to escape.

But in early European history, especially in the Anglo-Saxon countries, revenge could be entirely allayed through monetary remuneration. This *weregild* (*wergeld*) compensated the victim or his or her relatives for the harm done and that was the end of the matter, even if the crime was murder. The desire for revenge was not carried forth for years, decades, or centuries as it was with the Hatfields and McCoys in West Virginia and Kentucky or as it is even today among families or tribes in Pakistan, where the need for revenge can go on for a century, by which time the original causes of these blood feuds are probably forgotten.

Interestingly, the concept of *weregild* is carried over into both criminal and civil adjudication. In the former case, a fine may eliminate jail time; in the latter, compensatory and punitive monetary damages may allow a victim to release his or her anger and let the issue die*. This works well in western countries but not so much in Japan: I recall a case in which a man was harmed (his son may have been killed); he sued and won $15,000. His peers were aghast and bombarded him with complaints. He returned the money. The most horrible revenge scenario that I can envision is the case of a young teenager, who is bullied or disrespected at school and returns with his father's arsenal and murders innocent children. This occurs far too frequently. Of course, the destruction of the World Trade Center (very meaningful to me, because I grew up in its lee, just a few blocks away) is an extreme case of retribution for imagined national and/or religious harms. For some, retribution is the only form of justice that satisfies; here justice is qualifiedly fulfilled rather than denied. This is how Rosenbaum puts it: "Whether we admit it or not, whether we are permitted to act on it or not, revenge brings order to the moral universe…" (*Payback* 6). Rosenbaum draws an explicit distinction between legal fulfillment and moral justice. The law makes certain demands but the result is not always morally (i.e., ethically) just: "In choosing the law, one necessarily selects legal retribution over moral revenge" (Rosenbaum, *Payback* 20).

Revenge rebalances matters for victims, the moral universe, and book, television, and film readers and viewers. Those especially entranced by the subject should see *Retribution*, a 2023 Hollywood thriller, as well as *The Sting, Carrie, Taken,* and *Unforgiven,* among many other possibilities. (See directly below for related remarks.)

Philosophical Excursus

There exists a small clique of philosophers who inhabit ivory towers and create bizarre, misguided, and harmful theoretical structures. Because these folks, including, in the past, Schopenhauer, Nietzsche, and B. F. Skinner, and more recently, especially Bruce N. Waller as well as Galen Strawson, Derk Pereboom, and Gregg D. Caruso, insist that moral responsibility is an untenable myth, it is evident that they could not have anything to do with the procedures discussed in this study because perpetrators are not responsible for their actions and so they need not be punished. These scholars blame luck, genetics, the environment, that is, anything that will help to relieve individuals of taking (ethical) responsibility for what they do. Since this is the case, incarceration is an evil that must be avoided except in a small number of special cases where society must be protected from the likes of George Metesky (the mad bomber of the 1940s and 50s), Ted Kaczynski (the Unabomber), Charles Manson (murderer of some 35 people), or other socio- or psychopaths of whom there are many serial killers, cannibals, and madmen and women too.

Waller argues fairly and cogently for this position in *Against Moral Responsibility* and, surprisingly, unlike his colleagues, indicates that we do have free will, although causation is absolute. So we choose to act in a certain way but are not morally responsible for the result. This makes little sense, but Waller does not seem to care because he continues to churn out books and articles promoting this position. In an earlier study, *Freedom Without Responsibility*, free will was extinguished. Well, one only needs to recall that "A foolish consistency is the hobgoblin of little minds…."

It is neither constructive nor beneficial to argue with respected thinkers, scholars, doctors, lawyers, or even laymen who have convinced themselves that their ideas, beliefs, theories, and conspiracies are valid.

Philosophers, scientists, and medical personnel tell us that everything is determined, that we are living in a computer simulation, that consciousness does not exist, that our memories will be uploaded into computers, that we are visited by extraterrestrials, and that vaccines and masks are of no value during a pandemic. (See my *Debunking Scholarly Nonsense*.) The Wallerites insist that we cannot be held morally accountable and that it is impossible to assign reward or punishment, since we are not responsible for our actions. Here follows a hypothetical case that should convince readers that Waller's position is untenable: A newly permitted 16-year-old girl, with a fake ID, drinks herself into a stupor at a bar and eventually passes out; she awakes, goes to her car, and drives away. Sadly, she loses control and slams into a family killing the parents and their toddlers. She comes of an excellent family that has no history of mental illness; her parents spent years telling her that drinking and driving are socially unacceptable actions. She should be punished; the act is far too egregious for a court to let her off with a revoked license. It may seem harsh but she belongs in prison. (Almost 60 years ago, I had a student who accidentally killed her grandparents in a car accident; she should not be punished because this was not an irresponsible or purposeful act.) I wonder how Waller and company would deal with the Manson crew, Nazi murderers such as Himmler, Goebbels, Eichmann, Mengele, and Hitler. Were they alive, should they avoid punishment (retribution), since they are no longer threats to society?

In 2020, *Neuroethics* published a special issue devoted to "Justice Without Retribution." It features three of the four scholars mentioned above and argues for non-retributive justice, since the offenders are not morally responsible for their crimes and therefore should not be punished. Instead, solutions include "Benign Biological Interventions," "Biomedical Treatments," and forensics!

The Causes of All Our Troubles

There are four primary reasons for or causes of the injustice that permeates US society: inequity, religion, the confederacy, and states' rights. I am certain that this declaration will surprise and confuse readers but I hope to clarify matters without presenting a disquisition, one that could easily go on interminably.

Inequity manifests itself in many ways: racially, sexually, educationally, migrationally, and financially. Minorities, especially African Americans, are given a hard time when attempting to live in harmony with the majority population, which is sometimes bigoted, misogynistic, controlling, and hurtful. And so the more extremely fearful folks live in closed gated communities where it is quite difficult to become a member. Even Nixon, a disgraced US president, was partially refused entry into a New York coop; he had to live elsewhere. Sexuality plays an important role in social and legal settings. Things are better now for gay people, but transgender issues continue to haunt us especially in more conservative locations. Some educational institutions still have quota systems that disallow certain groups' members from matriculating, as was the case at Columbia for Jews early in the 20th century. Migration is currently a difficult and controversial subject but it is certainly unfair (unjust) to force normal people to wait in line at consulates and embassies around the world in order to attempt to enter the US legally with a valid visa, while half the population of central American countries, blighted by gangs of hoodlums, are on their way to cross our southern border unchecked. For land owners along the border as well as in other locations inundated by these folks, life is extremely difficult and dangerous. The US has a long history of embracing the downtrodden, but everyone in Myanmar or South Sudan cannot immigrate to a country, whose primary population (that is, not its billionaires) is already suffering financially.

Financial disparity is the single most pressing problem for most Americans. Whereas the capitalists and their stock holders generally do okay, the workers at Amazon, Starbucks, or Boeing have to strike to receive adequate pay at a time when inflation causes prices to soar. During the pandemic housing purchase costs doubled in some locations. New Yorkers would buy properties in Vermont sight unseen and for enormous sums. So, some people earned a profit and wealthy families were able to escape to the comparatively Covid-free countryside, but others were forced to remain in some areas earning subsistence pay. Two thirds of workers live paycheck to paycheck. This is reprehensible. Women earn less than men. Bank tellers are not remunerated well but the executives earn high salaries and bonuses. Some private bankers, at Goldman Sachs, earn hundreds of thousands of dollars each year and of course CEOs take home 15 million, while those who make the company profitable earn 32,000. Minorities are consistently underpaid. Migrants, legal or not, farm or construction workers, can be financially abused. And at times, very young children are forced to work in factories, and not just in Myanmar or Cambodia. This is a practice (child labor) defended by *Wall Street Journal* columnists!

Religion is difficult to criticize because so many people believe—in god, dogma, prayer, miracles, and practice. They are indoctrinated, (brainwashed) almost always into the beliefs of their parents, whether Daoist or Buddhist, Christian or Muslim. These beliefs are often unshakable and so progress on this front is impossible. The following anecdote will help those unfamiliar with religious fanaticism to understand: The chief rabbi of Amsterdam was released from a Nazi concentration camp. He sat down at a table and was asked whether he would like some cheese. After a long time without decent food, his reply was, Is it kosher! Unjust hatred, murder, war, devastation, and torture can all be traced to religious belief in Europe, the Americas, Africa, and the Near and Far East. Religion influences US law despite the Constitutional precept that disallows this.

The Confederacy was an aggregation of 11 southern slave holding states that seceded from the union primarily because they feared the abolition of slavery even before Lincoln issued the Emancipation Proclamation freeing plantation slaves who provided unpaid labor for those wealthy enough to purchase these people who were shipped over from Africa. It was an unjust system that should have been expunged through the Constitution, but since some of the founding fathers (Washington, Jefferson, Madison, inter alios) were slave owners, that was asking too much of those presumably entranced by *Liberté, égalité, and fraternité.* The Civil War that followed was a horrendous, violent, evil affair that cost as many as three quarters of a million military lives. Manumission did not end the problem. Reconstruction, Jim Crow, segregation, separate but equal, and southern attitude (racism) also took a toll. This attitude continues to do so. Many southerners still adulate the confederacy, which stands for oppression and injustice, and emplace statues (some of which have only recently been removed), wave flags, and affirm the secession as if it were praiseworthy, whereas it was seditious treason. This attitude, which has continued for 160 years, is physically, mentally, financially, and emotionally harmful to individuals residing in the south and to northerners who are sensitive to ongoing injustice. This naturally does not mean that everything is harmonious in Maine or Minnesota, New Mexico or Washington.

By the way, the Confederacy was of course preceded (and followed) by a segregationist attitude and national policy that allowed (insisted upon) discriminating against those who were not racially white. A superb example of this is the Daughters of the American Revolution (DAR) whose policy denied non-whites access to Constitution Hall as late as 1939, when Mahalia Jackson was forced to sing at the Lincoln Memorial because the DAR would not give permission for her to use their Hall. I know that this is the case because my sedentary mother, who almost never left New York City, took a bus to Washington, DC in order to hear and support Jackson and thereby human rights.

States rights may at first appear to be harmless bystanders, but in reality, much real injustice derives from the clash between individual states and the federal government. The situation was understandable in the distant colonial past but ludicrous today and especially when state laws are extremely divergent. The very earliest colonizers were fiercely independent; they formed enclaves, towns, cities, counties, and states. They were suspicious of government, since King George continually hassled and taxed them. The tea party led to a revolution after which the people were not likely to fully surrender rights to a federal government. The Tenth Amendment certifies this. And this is why a civil war was fought, as described above.

But today, no state law can compete with a similar federal statute. Here is how this operates: Some 60 years ago, I worked for the US Post Office from five pm until one am, when I was often asked to work for two more hours. Although New York State law disallows employers from forcing employees to work overtime, the federal government supersedes and one has no choice. At three am, I was once again asked to work two more hours but after ten hours even the federal government could not force me to continue. Sometimes I did; the pay was excellent.

This divergence allows individual states to license drivers at different ages; it allows older folks to drive with diminished eyesight; it allows DMVs to charge more or less to register a vehicle (in Oklahoma,` private tag agents charge an enormous amount for a new car and then each year this diminishes; in Vermont the cost for a car was always $76); it allows states to meddle with and in elections, gerrymandering and demanding various unreasonable things in order to vote; it allowed one state (Texas) to imprison pot smokers for 20 years, while another (Wisconsin, in specific cities) legalized its usage; it allows armaments and concealed weapons in some locations, while others do not. One of the most bizarre and unjust disparities is juridical jurisdiction: Many folks will recall how criminals (Bonnie and Clyde in a film) could cross a border (from Texas to Louisiana, for example), and then thumb their noses at the police chasers (although these robbers were eventually killed). State and local police have no authority outside their jurisdictions. And, until fairly recently, it of course allowed slavery and Jim Crow, segregation and mistreatment of minorities, especially African Americans. When Billie Holiday traveled in the South, she could not use the same restroom as her white band members nor could she eat with them in a restaurant; she had to hide on the bus.

Here is a recent example of how states enforce divergent laws some of which are beneficial, while others are unconstitutional, which leads one to wonder how they can get away with such evil. On June 26, 2024, *The New York Times* published an opinion piece in which Charles M. Blow described how Maryland's governor pardoned 175,000 drug offenders, seeking equity and justice. At the same time, Louisiana's governor signed bills that will "extend faith in public schools." This includes displaying the Ten Commandments in educational facilities (which is unconstitutional). There should be consistency and equity across state lines. Until there is, justice will remain curtailed.

Incredibly, we also have 574 native American tribes (with a total population under 10 million) and they are sovereign nations with their own laws and courts. Only a federal crime would be adjudicated in a federal court. Injustice follows. For example, in certain cases, if a non-tribal member has a child and then leaves the tribe (through divorce, for example), the child cannot also depart or if a non-tribal member outlives a spouse, he or she must leave the pueblo. Many of these nations issue their own license plates, disallow visitors and photography without the permission of elders with whom it may be difficult to meet, and other anomalies that rankle: Some tribal casinos only share minimal payments with members.

Federal legislators should work with reasonable state representatives, those who do not have an unwarranted committed loyalty to their states, in order to streamline federal legislation that would replace divergent state laws. Just how fanatical a commitment to one's state can be is exemplified by the following anecdote. In March of 1965, I was traveling on the Orient Express from Innsbruck to Istanbul, and then beyond. At one point, I stumbled upon a woman who was relaxing in a compartment. I was overjoyed: Wow, you are an American, I blurted out. No, she said; I am an Alaskan! So much for a federated country. Individual state sovereignty is as much of a hazard to a just American democracy as the election of an autocratic dictator.

Additional causes include two major anomalies: Congress and state lawmakers on the one hand and the Supreme Court on the other. This is most surprising, since these bodies should present the antithesis of harmful causation, but so many legislators care mainly about themselves and their often horrendous political parties and some of the Supreme justices are so unsavory, partisan, and corrupt that our democratic way of life is sorely threatened.

Legislators such as Theodore Bilbo, Pat McCarran, Joseph McCarthy, Bob Packwood, Ted Cruz, Marjorie Taylor Green, Elise Stefanik, and George Santos are so unsavory, so partisan, and at times so corrupt that they should be impeached but their colleagues will not act even when a peer belongs in prison.

The Supreme Court is "…corrupt, rotten and hurting America."
—Maureen Dowd

Over the centuries, there have been some extraordinary justices—John Marshall, Oliver Wendell Holmes, Jr., Louis Brandeis, William O. Douglas, Ruth Bader Ginsburg—and even when one disagrees with their rulings, she can still respect them. This is no longer the case. Americans are dissatisfied with the Supreme Court and with good reason. Jesse Wegman puts it this way: "…[T]oday's court… is finding new ways to embarrass itself, thanks largely to the brazen behavior of two of its most senior members, Justices Samuel Alito and Clarence Thomas, who are making a mockery of their obligation to at least appear neutral and independent. They fail to report large gifts, luxury vacations and payments to their family members by wealthy donors, at least one of whom had business before the court, and they express nakedly partisan opinions or fail to adequately distance themselves when their spouses express such views." He further insists that they are probably breaking the law. For example, Alito flew the US flag upside down and refuses to recuse himself when appropriate. The consensus is that the court is corrupt and out of control. Some call for Congress to do something about the situation but the justices deny Congressional authority and in any case, the legislators do nothing.

Thus, justice is often denied to those seeking redress in the highest court in the land. Extraordinarily, some justices agree: Sonia Sotomayor gets so frustrated with her colleagues' decisions that she despairs, returns to her chambers and cries, hoping that equality, diversity, and justice return to the court (VanSickle). On July 2, 2024, *The New York Times* ran an opinion piece by the emeritus Harvard law professor Lawrence H. Tribe with the following headline: "The Supreme Court's Immunity Decision is an Outrage." Indeed, it is and for purely political rather than legal reasons, and so "The three liberal justices—Sonia Sotomayor, Elena Kagan and Ketanji Brown Jackson—sharply criticized the majority's opinion in *scathing* dissents" (Richer) See especially David Brock's *Stench: The Making of the Thomas Court and the Unmaking of America.*

International Law

One of the things that most Americans, even those involved with the law, do not realize is that legal education and processes are radically different even in democracies closely related to the US such as England and Wales, where barristers and solicitors have very different legal responsibilities. When I was a student at the University of Innsbruck, 60 years ago, my roommate studied law. Among his classes was *Kirchenrecht*, canon law, the law of the church. Since Austria is a Catholic country and the separation of church and state does not exist in the same absolute way that it does in the US, lawyers must take into account canon law. Many continental countries including France and Germany have some form of plea bargaining, probation and parole, but not bail bonding. So things play out differently for the accused even in other democracies. One may well imagine how these processes fail (or do not exist) in repressive countries such as Myanmar, North Korea, Syria, South Sudan, Cuba, or Libya.

I take France as an exemplar of continental law and briefly discuss its workings in the following chapters where appropriate. But France (and its Napoleonic Code which emphasizes civil rather than case law) do not necessarily reflect the EU situation in every case, since there are 27 diverse lands, and this is so despite the general legal system of the EU, which, by the way, takes precedence over individual countries' laws. Indeed, some EU countries do not even use the Euro. And so their laws on parole or incarceration, for example, may differ, sometimes dramatically. Japan is the second country I include here.

Note that a few lands (Iran, North Korea, Saudi Arabia) insist that one is guilty until proven innocent, the antithesis of English common law and the laws of the EU lands.

Five Final Remarks

Migrants

In the past, in order to emigrate from another country to the US, one had to visit an embassy or consulate and request a visa based on a variety of necessities: skills needed in the US; relations such as spouses; desire for a better life; asylum. Sometimes, the borders were open and lots of people arrived. At other times, the US had a strong isolationist policy and it denied requests, especially when an actual or implied quota system was in effect—and so, for example, Chinese or Jews were excluded. Very few people migrated illegally across borders. More recently, Central American countries such as Honduras, Nicaragua, and El Salvador but also Venezuela, all wracked by internal dissension, political madness, and gangs, have forced a substantial percentage (many millions) of their populations (as well as people from other lands) to walk across hundreds of miles, reach Mexico, and continue to the US border in Texas, Arizona, New Mexico, and California where they cross the Rio Grande and ignore other impediments such as walls, border patrols, deserts, and local landowners and either die, are captured, or reach safety.

This entire fiasco is an affront to justice. No matter what result occurs, justice is denied. Sadly, there is no fair solution to this crisis, since the third world is such a mess and it is natural for people to wish to escape (from Africa, South America, or South Asian dictatorships) to a better life in Europe or North America). Although critics are disenchanted with the severe US policy of rejecting some aspirants (recall the horrible policy of separating children from their parents), it is good to recall that the US also does allow some (many) migrants to stay—in hotels in New York City—and eventually many will become US citizens. Other lands are not so generous: It is very difficult to become a Swiss citizen and almost impossible in Japan; Koreans have lived there for generations and have never acquired citizenship.

Juveniles

This study concerns adult offenders. Occasionally, I cite research that covers juveniles because it is relevant to the matter under discussion. Juveniles guilty of heinous crimes should be treated in similar fashion (tried as adults, for example). Some youngsters have gone so far in the wrong direction that the chances of rehabilitation are highly improbable. When I was about 12, a fellow gang member (of the same age) was so mean, malicious, and harmful that I predicted he would end up in jail. Many years later, I learned that he was serving time in a maximum security prison. I am not a draconian retributionist and I sympathize with young children who have had difficult lives, but once a deed is committed (armed robbery, assault, especially wanton murder), which occurs far too frequently, sympathy is the wrong response. The message given is, Hey, I am only 13; I got away with it; I can again. No teenager earning almost two thousand dollars a week transporting or selling drugs (which should be legalized, for which see below) will be willing to work for $15 an hour. On the other hand, those juveniles who have merely strayed, abjured violence, not seriously harmed, and appear to be rehabilitatable, can take advantage of current probation and parole programs—until they are curtailed, but those convicted of heinous acts should be imprisoned for life without a chance of parole. The lower and Supreme Courts are always interested in the rights of the criminal and tend to ignore or downplay the rights of and harms to the victim, and so life without parole for juveniles is considered cruel and unusual punishment. But consider the appalling case of Rashaun Weaver, who was 14 when he murdered Tessa Majors, a Barnard student, by stabbing her. Majors is dead, but Weaver was sentenced to a mere 14 years to life (https://people.com/crime/final-teen-involved-barnard-student-tessa-majors-murder-sentenced/). He will soon be paroled for good behavior! Is this fair recompense for taking a young person's life? Is justice truly served here?

The 14-year-old boy who killed four people and wounded nine in Georgia in 2024 had easy access to arms, which implicates his parents. These ongoing shootings have little effect on legislators who succumb to the NRA's influence. But true reform is mandatory if these heinous actions are to be curtailed. Concerning the shooter, should he be bailed, plea-bargained, probated, or paroled? In a different era, his age would have been irrelevant and he would have been executed. It is most unfair to his victims to sentence him to life in prison and then parole him, a rehabilitated man, a dozen years later. Cf. Miller v. Alabama but also Bassett v. Arizona.

Felons

Violent felons (robbers, muggers, assailants, predators, sexual abusers, rapists, kidnappers, and murderers) should never be bailed, bonded, plea bargained, probated, or paroled. The recidivism rate and the risk to recent and new victims is far too high. And yet all of these offenders may be offered these benefits through leniency and expediency. At times, court ordered punishments are so indulgent, so off base that the entire country erupts in anger. This occurred when a Stanford University student was found guilty of rape, received a six month sentence, and subsequently was released early. Rape is one of the vilest of crimes and should be legally treated in the same way that murder is (which often is far too kindly).

Judges' Discretion

Problems with court procedures and rules can cause real misery: Allowable witness questioning is subject to absolutist rules but judges, for example, have the discretion to disallow a witness at a hearing or trial to speak at length and to only answer in monosyllables, which can be extremely misleading. Consider that a teenage girl might be asked whether she did indeed stab the victim. When she says Yes, but…, the judge cuts her off so that the court does not learn that the victim had ripped off her dress, was strangling her, and was attempting to rape her. To pursue her account, against the judge's admonition, is to risk contempt of court, which may entail a fine or jail.

Clemency and Pardons

A final problematic area is local, gubernatorial, or presidential clemency (reprieves, commutations) but especially pardons often granted not because of legal failure but rather because of political machination such as large financial contributions. A pardon should not be tendered to an innocent person. He or she should be exonerated. A pardon is appropriate for certain individuals who appear to deserve it for some reason but not because they or their siblings donate to a politician or his PAC. This abrogation is exemplified by Clinton's pardon of Marc Rich and others' abusive actions pardoning miscreants, whereas Biden issued only eleven pardons until he was about to leave office. Other presidents have pardoned hundreds or even thousands of people but there are many legitimate reasons for this.

See <https://en.wikipedia.org/wiki/List_of_people_pardoned_or_granted_clemency_by_the_president_of_the_United_States> for a complete rundown of presidential pardons.

Note: I have never been able to understand nor empathize with the payment of money in exchange for a human life. I know of an instance in which someone died, a suit was brought, and the recompense was divided among many relatives. I would not share in such a reward. Rosenbaum informs us that many Holocaust victims refuse to take any "restitution payments from Germany" because it would be like taking blood money and allow the German people to mitigate their guilt (*Payback* 174).

Part One
Major Problems

Chapter One: Bail/Bonding

Besides arrest, bail is the most important criminal justice decision made today.
—Shima Baradaran Baughman

Definition

Bail for pretrial release is a monetary payment made to a court in order to ensure that a suspect, an alleged criminal, will show up for a hearing or trial. No bail is assessed for minor crimes such as traffic infractions, although if a driver were to travel 90 miles an hour in a school zone, a judge might very well demand bail. The amount of money involved varies from $50 to as much as a million. (The record is three billion!). Bail laws vary from state to state.

If the amount is small, a person will put up the bail him- or herself. When the demanded bail is out of reach for the accused, a bail bondsman may be willing to furnish the money based on some form of collateral such as the accused's home or car or coin collection. (Sometimes, a parent or offspring will provide the bail or collateral.) The percentage provided by the accused is eventually kept by the bondsman for his sometimes outlandish fee. Anyone familiar with courthouses in large urban areas will have noticed nearby stores with "Bail Bonds" inscribed on their windows. Only the US and the Philippines allow this detrimental system to operate. No matter what is mooted, said, explained, discussed, or attempted, there are always people who in one way or another cannot afford bail. These many poor, indigent, or homeless folks end up in jail. This is neither useful, economical, nor just.

Besides cash, there exist many types of bail including surety bond, recognizance, unsecured, percentage, citation release, and property bond. These and other forms are discussed at length in "Bail in the United States," a *Wikipedia* article that, naturally, offers a detailed history, legal overview, and critique. When cash is demanded, it must not be overwhelming, since the Eighth Amendment to the Constitution specifically prohibits this: "Excessive bail shall not be required...." Nevertheless, it does occur that inordinate, indeed, impossible amounts are demanded, in one notorious case, three billion dollars, later reduced to a mere five million; this homicidal maniac, Robert Durst, should not have been released under any circumstances.

To disabuse those who think that bail and bonding are simple, straight forward affairs, I suggest they consult the *Bail Bond Handbook,* a 142-page magnum opus, published in 2023 by the Texas Association of Counties. It covers bonds for witnesses, order for emergency protection, disbursements from county fund, and a plethora of other subtleties (Davis).

Benefits

Naturally, there exist beneficial aspects to bail (although some scholars disagree). A person can avoid spending time in jail or prison, which can be both very unpleasant and unsafe. A major benefit for the alleged perpetrator is that it gives him or her the opportunity to escape. This, however, is a detriment to society, if the person were to disappear into the Mojave Desert or abscond to Costa Rica, which in the past did not have an extradition treaty with the US. And Somalia, Vietnam, Ecuador and Venezuela, for example, do not extradite. Even today, with facial recognition, smart passports, and other technological systems, a wealthy person could arrange an escape to South America or the Near East (with a false passport and beard or on his own plane or yacht, for example). Someone facing an assured 30-year prison sentence might prefer to live in Kuwait rather than in Leavenworth, Folsom, or Attica. It also allows family members to feel relief rather than anxiety. Pretrial release ostensibly protects various actors from threats and danger.

For those who require bail or a bond and wish to traverse the alleyways with dexterity and fore-knowledge (this is quite improbable), see S. J. Plotkin's *Get Bail, Leave Jail,* which offers advice on queries to ask a bondsman, types of collateral, working with court procedures, and other formalities. Others may wish to become a bondsman or woman and there are many guides to starting a business. Still others may be enticed by a historical perspective, how things were done hundreds of years ago, and for them there is *A Digest of the Doctrine of Bail in Civil and Criminal Cases,* A. Highmore Jr.'s 1783 detailed overview of eighteenth-century Britain's legal machinations. A historical overview of bail in the US is just part of *The Bail Book,* Shima Baradaran Baughman's comprehensive study that covers crime prediction, costs, race, terrorism, and other salient topics. These and many other valuable volumes are accessible (at times in full text) through *Google Books* rather than on *Project Gutenberg,* which is not very useful in this context.

Detriments

As far back as a hundred years ago, bail bonding was extremely lucrative because of high bail necessities and ever more defendants who could not pay their own bail: "The corrupt and sometimes abusive practices of bail bondsmen [eventually] became the focus of inquiries" (Billings 1352). So, there obviously are many detriments to bail and therefore Illinois, New Jersey, New Mexico, New York and Washington, DC do not allow it. Justice is not served if the wealthy or those who have some form of collateral can avoid jail time and continue with their lives unaffected, whereas those who have no financial resources whatsoever will be forced to await trial in jail. If readers have been following historical developments over the past 400 years, they know precisely who is affected by this injustice: the homeless, poor, minorities, and especially African Americans. (Persons of color are imprisoned at a much higher rate than white folks, although this has been diminishing for African Americans.)

There is also something seedy about the process of bail bonding; it seems to be akin to borrowing from a loan shark. In both cases, one is caught in a financial trap, needs money immediately, and so is willing to make certain sacrifices: Pay a fee to remain at large or offer an enormous, usurious rate of interest to someone who is willing to provide funds when a bank is not. Bondsmen put up the money in order to earn an excellent profit. In reality, matters are much worse: In a 1964 monograph, Daniel J. Freed and Patricia M. Wald point out that the bonding system is replete with corruption, abuse, and collusion: At times, the court, the police, and organized crime are all involved (34). Almost 60 years later, a *Fact Sheet: Profit Over People* report reconfirms the horrors of bail/bonding: "Rife with unethical and harmful practices, the commercial bail industry maximizes profits at the expense of safety and justice." Furthermore, "Reliance on cash bail results in racially and economically unjust outcomes, high rates of pretrial incarceration, increased costs to taxpayers, and negative public safety consequences" (Preston et al.). Reform is constantly considered; therefore, if so many critics over such an extended period complain about a harmful system, why are major alterations not undertaken nationally through federal legislation or locally in every state? The answer, naturally, lies in the capitalist market system, greed, commercialization, profit, lobbying, and all of the paraphernalia that allows Congress, state legislators, and the Supreme Court to prostitute justice in the name of a conservative and ubiquitously harmful agenda as well as a financially powerful industry, one that earns more than two billion dollars a year. And keep in mind the fact that the system operates differently in different states, which means that "justice" is allocated in a variety of ways depending on where a crime is committed and who the perpetrator is: The elite, wealthy, and non-minorities are often treated differently than the poor, homeless, vagrants, and minorities, especially African Americans. Illegal aliens (undocumented immigrants) have their own problems.

A successful contract with a bail bondsman is more complicated than I have indicated and can result in some very unsavory actions, the most harrowing of which is the possibility that a bondsman's agent, a bounty hunter, may locate a bail jumper, legally enter a home, and arrest the person. If there is resistance, it is possible that physical harm or even death may ensue. Indeed, this has occurred and it is a very sad ending to an agreement between the accused and a bail bondsman. Shannon M. Baker and her colleagues present an excellent overview of the legal and illegal activities of these "quasi-criminal justice officials" who commit "extra-legal violence and constitutional rights violations" (abstract).

The worst aspect to bail (bonded or not) is that it allows an alleged criminal to walk free, when he or she should be incarcerated. Naturally, if the person is innocent, the following does not obtain, but if truly guilty, money should not be the key to freedom. An alleged embezzler, assailant, or murderer should not be allowed to wander in offices or streets and harm again. Of course, in the US, we are innocent until proven guilty, but a person such as Bernie Madoff, accused of a massive fraud, was known to be guilty before trial. Should he be given the opportunity to disappear just because he has some remnant of the 65 billion dollars he was at first alleged to have stolen, bilking even his "friend" Elie Wiesel. (The 65 billion was later reduced to 20 billion.) He was a monster without a conscience. Lock him up! (Readers may recall that his son committed suicide. Had he not died in prison before his 150-year term was up, he probably would have been paroled for good behavior!) Robert Durst harmed a lot of people. His bail was set at three billion dollars! If he had paid this extraordinary amount of money and then once again jumped bail, would justice have been served? Money should not be a substitute for justified punishment. When a crime is horrendous or when there is a legitimate flight risk, bail should be denied.

Various urban jurisdictions (and states) treat bail differently and some have been interested in reforming the system, the details of which are laid out in a series of chapters in Paul B. Wice's 1974 study *Freedom for Sale*. A possible if radical solution that I envision and that at first may appear at least to some well-intentioned people as untenable, is that many alleged minor criminals can be released on their own recognizance. Should they fail to show up for their trials, especially if they are accused of serious legal breaches, the penalty should be severe. Most people will not be willing to serve an extra ten years in prison for this failure. What this amounts to is a very severe contempt of court. Instituting such changes is very difficult, but since some states have eliminated bail, positive alterations are possible.

Here follow some remarks on state variation: "The key differences in bail regulations across states extend beyond the use of cash bail to include aspects such as bail bond agent licensing requirements, the allowable fees and premiums that bail bondsmen can charge, and the protections afforded to defendants in the bail process. Some states strictly regulate the bail bond industry, imposing caps on the fees that can be charged and requiring detailed contracts that outline the terms of the bail agreement. Others may offer more leeway, resulting in a wide range of practices within the industry" ("Navigating"). What this means is that if one murders someone in New Hampshire, reasonable bail may be possible, whereas, say, in Louisiana, one may spend an eternity in pre-trial arrest, if a million-dollar bail is unavailable.

Now here follows a list of cases in which the wealthy jumped bail along with an occasional intercalated comment. Those readers who keep up to date with the news and criminal activity will recognize some of these miscreants.

"10 Super Rich Guys Who Jumped Bail" [Eight are listed here.]

Roman Polanski. Crime: Statutory rape.

Polanski is the famous film director who long ago made *Knife in the Water, Rosemary's Baby, Chinatown,* and *Tess of the D'Urbervilles,* for which he insisted that Nastassja Kinski cut her long hair. Very sadly, his wife Sharon Tate was murdered by Manson lunatics. None of this has anything to do with the accusation of statutory rape of a 13-year-old child in 1977 that he admitted was valid. He jumped bail and lived abroad for many years; he has been free of US jurisdiction for almost half a century. A trial date in 2025 is set.

Marcus Schrenker. Crime: Fraud.

Christopher Skase. Crime: Embezzlement.

Robert Vesco. Crime: Fraud and profiteering.

This joker stole 224 million dollars in 1972 and jumped bail; he ended up in the Bahamas and finally died in 2008.

Marc Rich. Crime: Tax evasion.

Rich is another well-known bail jumper who spent the following years in luxury in Switzerland and Spain. He was pardoned by Clinton—because of his political donations.

Yuan Hongwei. Crime: Counterfeit.

Norman Y. Hsu. Crime: Fraud.

This bizarre character jumped bail, returned to the US, and jumped bail again! The judge apparently did not learn anything from the first occurrence.

Rakesh Saxena. Crime: Embezzlement (Lubin).

Also see the following: <https://www.spatzlawfirm.com/blog/2022/10/most-high-profile-bail-bond-cases-in-us-history/> for some unusual cases that resulted in both high bail (120 million to three billion dollars) but additionally that indicate the horrible things these people did: murder, brothel ownership, and securities fraud.

Bail and its sibling bonding are superfluous and should be universally eliminated. Justice is not served when a person such as Marc Rich does not have to pay for his crime nor for his bail indiscretion. "Studies dissecting the bail system have been conducted for a good many years. Their uniform conclusion is that the system has not worked very well" (Freed 110). Even worse, "Some sixty-five years ago [noted in 1988] a study directed by Roscoe Pound and Felix Frankfurter referred to professional bondsmen as \'parasites\' and to their activities as \'tending to prostitute the administration of justice in the inferior courts\'" (Devine).

Not surprisingly, a host of documentaries (e.g., *Inside America's For-Profit Bail System*) as well as Hollywood films (e.g., *One for the Money* and *The Hunter*) depict the seedy side of bail bonding and bounty hunting. And even novelists have lent a hand here: See Robert J. C. Stead's *The Bail Jumper (*1914) and R L Goldman's *Out on Bail* (1937). What is surprising is the astonishing number of bail bond videos that are available on *YouTube,* well over 400 of them*;* it appears as if every bondsman and bondswoman has a video advertising their services. Additional videos cover how to become a bond agent and the murders of bail jumpers as well as bondsmen.

Reforms and Alternatives

The reformation of bail and bonding has frequently been discussed, analyzed, and proposed but with only limited success. As indicated above, some states have eliminated both, but they still exist in the others. It is bad enough that a foolish person has committed a minor misdemeanor or a major felony and must suffer the physical, mental, and emotional consequences associated with the deed. Add to this the judicial proceedings and the harsh sentence that may be handed down and few normal people, even hardened criminals, will not find themselves in a state of agitated anxiety. Now comes the extreme misery of dealing with a judge's bail order. This derives from a game the defense lawyer and the prosecutor play before the judge (or another person). The lawyer claims that his socially exemplary killer does not present a flight risk, whereas the prosecutor points out that the accused has been arrested 27 times and will undoubtedly flee to Bolivia, no matter how high the bail is set. Taking all of the hyperbole into account, the judge must make a Solomonic decision assigning a reasonable sum in order to protect both the accused and the state. The victim? Well, she does not really matter here, does she? Additionally, there is the probable necessity of working with a bondsman. Some folks will end up hospitalized. When bail is not an option for the indigent, the person may be jailed, the result of which can be catastrophic personally and nationally: "The bail system contributes to the United States' high rate of incarceration. An estimated two-thirds of the 750,000 people in the nation's jails are awaiting resolution of their cases; as such, they are legally innocent" (Wylie).

In 1976, Wayne H. Thomas published *Ball Reform in America*, in which he offers an explication of what he terms an irrational and inequitable system. He begins with a historical overview of mooted reforms, especially those of the early 1960s, such as the Manhattan Bail Project. Subsequently, bail projects were created in some 60 locations across the country. The rest of the book discusses procedural details, e.g., failure to appear, deposit bail plans, the police role, and many other features. Now, 50 years later, as so much time and energy, including Congressional hearings, have been allocated to reform, we are still demanding payment from the indigent who must spend time in jail because they cannot meet bail requirements. (The profound interest in reform is so extensive that *Google Books* produces some 500 hits, although many items are not entirely relevant.)

Jessica Brand and Jessica Pishko begin their detailed explanation of bail reform with two brief anecdotes. This is the second: For stealing seven dollars and a bottle of perfume [and threatening], Kennth Humphrey spent a year in jail, because he could not meet the $350,000 bail requirement! This is insane: Why was bail demanded in this case and why was it set at this exorbitant amount? This is reminiscent of Jean Valjean's punishment in *Les Misérables:* He spent 19 years in jail for stealing a loaf of bread and trying to escape. But Hugo's account is dated 1862, whereas Humphrey's bail was set in 2017, more than 150 years later, which shows how little progress has been made. And note that there is "...a correlation between pretrial detention and both conviction and recidivism." So those jailed (and for no good reason) are likely to eventually be found guilty and then return to a life of crime.

Although virtually all commentators indicate that the system is in dire need of reform or elimination, an occasional iconoclast insists that we should hold back, and so it is with V. L. Williams who in 1978 discusses "Nine Reasons to Go Slow on Bail Bond Reform." These include the following: The government should not disrupt this industry because it earns money, the change will cost more, bail money is useful, and defendants will delay court appearances (abstract). This defense of the industry seems reasonable if one is a capitalist bail bondsman. Otherwise, costs and payments are the last reasons to maintain a harmful (and at times unconstitutional) system.

Finally, in 2021, Isabella Jorgensen and Sandra Susan Smith published "The Current State of Bail Reform in the United States: Results of a Landscape Analysis of Bail Reforms Across All 50 States," which offers many insights on the ways in which reform is taking place. This Harvard Working Paper summarizes the ways in which reforms may occur: These include alterations in court rules and opinions on bail; prosecutors' refusals to issue bail; and city, county, and state legislature changes. The authors include a chart that lays out the precise changes that have occurred in various states, e.g., alteration of pretrial service programs in Montana and New Jersey or setting a bail ceiling in Vermont as well as many others (2-7). This paper contains additional valuable observations on the reform process, impacts of reform, and risk assessment tools (passim). (Some critics claim that risk assessment in this context has negative results because it is racially biased.)

See Max Travers and his five co-authors' *Rethinking Bail: Court Reform or Business as Usual?* For the ways in which bail is being handled in Australia.

Minor Reforms

Since bail may not prevent a person from jumping and thus avoiding a trial and when a person cannot raise bail, he or she is jailed which costs taxpayers millions of dollars, some minor changes can be implemented, although the bail bonding industry objects to any alteration that would impinge on its ability to earn money. Allie Preston includes "Increasing investments in pretrial services" and "Ensuring counsel at first appearance." Additionally, "The Bail Project [BP] is a 501(c)(3) nonprofit organization with dozens of locations across the United States. We can only offer bail assistance in cities where we have a local branch." It insists that "Bail is not what makes people return to court." And so for the poor, the BP will pay bail and it does not require repayment; it also strives to remove "money from justice" (The Bail Project).

Major Reforms

Problems with bail and bonding are so evident and yet radical elimination has not occurred everywhere. Here are two suggestions from Thanithia Billings: "Law and public policy compels courts to secure bail only to the extent that it will guarantee a defendant's appearance in court. This Note argues that in order to accomplish this, two important changes must occur. First, commercial bail bonds should be eliminated in favor of a system in which cash bail is not the default method of securing pretrial release. Second, all states should establish and maintain pretrial services agencies that aid courts in making bail determinations" (1337). In "Toward an Optimal Bail System," a typical 95-page law review *article,* one that is overwhelmed with 302 at times superfluous footnotes, Crystal S. Yang presents yet another historical overview of bail bonding and then proceeds to cover many aspects of this oppressive necessity, which we cannot seem to expunge. English common law favors precedent and yet we no longer hang malefactors and we claim to maintain humane prison conditions (which we often do not). Consider that Judge Aileen Cannon ignored all previous precedents by dismissing the classified documents case against Donald Trump; so it is possible to change; it just requires ignoring the powerful bail bonding industry lobby, which stifles every attempt at improvement*. "Bail reform [Yang concludes] is on the horizon and the consequences of any reform are likely extensive, as reforms to our existing bail system have the potential to affect the millions of defendants who are detained every year before trial" (1492). She proposes a cost-benefit framework which can improve equity, the result of which is that electronic monitoring is preferable to pre-trial detention (1399).

Similar in intent and structure to Yang is Alexa Van Brunt and Locke E. Bowman's "Toward a Just Model of Pretrial Release: A History of Bail Reform and a Prescription for What's Next," a 75 page paper adorned with 377 notes. Here, the authors insist that "The decision whether to release a defendant prior to trial is, in the great majority of cases, the most consequential ruling that will occur in the case—in terms of its effect on the defendant's life, on his or her family, on his or her future prospects, and on the particular case in which the defendant stands charged. At this moment in history, there is widespread revulsion toward the unnecessary cruelty of a system that depends far too heavily on incarceration. We should not squander the moment by demanding less than what justice requires" (774). Furthermore, "Reformers must not lose sight of the bottom line: we seek a system in which pretrial liberty actually is the norm and the number of persons detained is dwarfed by the vast majority who are granted liberty. Some risk to public safety is necessarily associated with this model. But the assumption of that risk is essential if practice is to conform to constitutional principles of due process, equal protection, and the presumption of innocence" (771-772). No one, except bail bondsmen and bounty hunters, could fail to agree with all of these authors.

Similar legal discussion has been carried on for centuries both in the US and the UK but improvement is elusive. Nevertheless, Congress has considered or enacted various editions of the *Bail Bond Fairness Act* (1997, 2003, 2007). Illinois' experiment in eliminating bail through the Pretrial Fairness Act (PFA) soon resulted in the saving of many millions of dollars in bail payments; defendants' freedom is no longer dependent on payment for electronic monitoring; and statewide consistency has increased. The PFA seems to be a success (Stemen). In 2018, California passed a law eliminating cash bail. The American Bail Coalition fought back and in 2020, the state repealed the new law (Hernández). It is very difficult to make progress when powerful lobbying groups stifle change in order to enhance usurious profits. Interestingly, bail bonding companies publish diatribes on the internet defending their existence. Better is the following: "... [T]he Harris County Criminal Courts at Law approved a landmark settlement proposal—Rule 9.1—that requires mandatory release of close to 85 percent of people arrested on misdemeanor charges in the county" (New York's). This is excellent progress against bail but it concerns a single Texas county and its limited number of incarcerated. In 2017, the Chicago prosecutor indicated that his office would not require bail for minor crimes (Brand). Many other locales are making similar adjustments but this is why states (as well as county and city) rights are so harmful: These alterations must take place on a national level for which see below.

Radical Reforms

These can only come from Congressional fiat, one that *fully eliminates* bail, bonding, bondsmen, and the bonding industry. To expect individual states to do so in a consistent manner is asking too much. It is as if a federal crime such as treason were treated differently depending on the venue. For example, if the Rosenbergs had lived in Nevada or Missouri, would they have been given life sentences with no chance of parole, and then released 30 years later instead of being executed? The answer is No! State law does not supersede federal legislation. For some, the elimination of money bail is but the beginning: They also demand release of the non-violent incarcerated because they lack the ability to post bail.

International Law

Bail bonding does not exist in France. Indeed, as indicated above, only the US and the Philippines allow this detrimental system to operate. In Japan, bail may be requested and granted unless the crime is extremely serious. The bail money is returned after the trial concludes (https://www.courts.go.jp/english/judicial_sys/FAQ_on_criminal_procedure/index.html).

Note: I might remark that the entire lobbying system which so influences Congress—through political donations—should also be eliminated. It is ironic that the Constitution gives individuals the First Amendment right "to petition the Government for a redress of grievances," although that does not really occur, but powerful groups are able to successfully lobby Congress. This entire business is corrupt.

Chapter Two: Plea Bargaining

An Unnecessary Evil

Definition

When a prosecutor wishes to expedite a case, even a serious felony such as first degree murder, he or she will try to make a deal with the accused by offering a reduced sentence. This saves time, energy, money, and a jury trial. When the evidence weighs heavily against the accused, a lawyer may advise that one should agree to a lesser charge and therefore a lesser sentence and so a guilty plea would be the best choice. At times, a judge may reject the agreement. Copping a plea (as the slang expression goes) does not further justice. Indeed, of all of the procedures etc. criticized in this monograph, plea bargaining is the most destructively unjust for it allows someone who has acted egregiously to get away without paying a fair and just price; the punishment no longer fits the crime. Note that, astonishingly, of all federal convictions, 98% result from bargaining; the figure for state convictions is 95%. Plea bargaining is implemented in criminal cases; in civil cases, settlements, similarly, are advocated. They too are breaches of true justice.

The insane twists and turns of the law, accepted and affirmed by lower courts and even the (politicized) Supreme Court (including immunity for a president) can be found in the Alford Case: "*The Court allowed the guilty plea with a simultaneous protestation of innocence* only because there was enough evidence to show that the prosecution had a strong case for a conviction and the defendant was entering such a plea to avoid this possible sentencing..." which would have resulted in his execution (https://en.wikipedia.org/wiki/Alford_plea#:~:text=The%20Alford%20guilty%20plea%20is,first%2Ddegree%20murder%20in%201963). And then there is the complex case of Alec Baldwin, who *accidentally* killed a person on the set of *Rust*, a film being shot in New Mexico. First, know that premeditated murderers can plead to a lesser crime; second, Baldwin did not know the gun was loaded; third, the armorer was found guilty of involuntary manslaughter, because she was responsible for the gun's condition; fourth, I do not understand why Baldwin was accused of a crime (he used the gun as a pointer?) when this was an accident, similar in intent to a car mishap in which someone is killed, but no one is charged; fifth, *he was allowed to plea bargain but, bizarrely, this misdemeanor plea was later revoked and he was charged with a felony;* finally, in a truly outlandish conclusion, the case was dismissed because the prosecutor withheld evidence. (See <https://www.nytimes.com/live/2024/07/10/arts/alec-baldwin-rust-trial> and <https://www.nytimes.com/2024/07/12/arts/rust-trial-pause-alec-baldwin-shooting.html?searchResultPosition=2> among many other possibilities, for more details.). By the way, for some inexplicable reason, this anomalous case appeared to be so crucial that it was broadcast live on Court TV. Pleading to a lesser crime is always a travesty, as is much that obtains in our legal and juridical systems. As for Baldwin, he should not have been charged at all and dismissing on a technicality also does not serve justice. Civil suits are another story. Always recall that "…In 2012, the Supreme Court said that 'plea bargaining… is not some adjunct to the criminal justice system; it is the criminal justice system'" (Trivedi citing the Supreme Court).

At first glance, plea bargaining appears to be a simple process, but when dealing with American Law, nothing is straightforward. See < https://barkanresearch.com/top-plea-bargaining-cases/> for ten cases that influence how plea bargains are adjudicated.

Benefits

Plea bargaining saves time and money. The court calendars are so jammed that a case may not come up for a really long time. It also allows the accused to plead guilty to a lesser crime (even when innocent, though this is not really acceptable) and thus be given a lesser punishment; so it is beneficial to the defendant, although this is a disservice to justice. Consider the plea deal reached in July 2024 with Khalid Sheikh Mohammed (and others), the person accused of masterminding the 9/11 massacre, perhaps the most egregious deal ever foisted on the justice system: He will thereby avoid the death penalty, but families of those murdered are extremely upset by this abrogation of justice (Liebermann). And JD Vance had this reaction: We "Need a president who kills terrorists, not negotiates with them." But wait:

Not surprisingly, two days later, the Defense Secretary revoked the deal, which had been called "a revolting abdication of the government's responsibility to defend America and provide justice." The death penalty is once again a possibility, but a trial will not take place in the near future (Rosenberg). This case continues to evolve.

Although virtually all commentators deride plea bargaining, an occasional scholar offers a different perspective. In *Plea Bargaining's Triumph,* George Fisher presents a univocal panegyric to this procedure: "Plea Bargaining may be, as some chroniclers claim, the invading barbarian. But it has won all the same" (1) and this is because "It pushed aside the indeterminate sentence, and it supported those institutions, such as probation and the public defender, that aided its cause" (230). Most people are not convinced.

Detriments

Plea Bargaining has been called "An unnecessary evil." Rosenbaum insists that "Plea arrangements undermine truth and subvert justice" (*Myth* 100). For the defendant, it remains unclear whether it is truly advantageous to him or her, and sometimes an innocent person may plead guilty in order to facilitate matters and avoid a trial. The speedy trial guaranteed by the Constitution is something of a myth. The Speedy Trial Act mandates that it must occur within 70 days but it often takes nine months and may linger for years. Consider the many criminal and civil cases filed against Donald Trump that have lingered in part because of appeals and other legal maneuvers. Neither the government nor the defendant has the right to confuse or impair the system by delaying trials. And it is not just individual malefactors who are manipulated into plea deals. This headline, "U.S. Said to Seek Boeing Guilty Plea to Avoid Trial in 737 Max Crashes," to a June 2024 *New York Times* article, coming many years after the accidents, makes it clear that the government prefers a ca. 244 million dollar fine and some oversight to a trial for fraud. The victims' families are aghast and call the deal "outrageous" because Boeing would not be forced to admit fault in the deaths of 346 people (Chokshi).

In *Plea Bargaining,* Milton Heumann concludes that "For the most part, new judges, prosecutors, and defense attorneys are not well prepared for their jobs in the court." They therefore mistakenly believe that plea bargaining should be used in only extreme cases (153).

But Heumann is wrong. In their ingenuousness, these officers of the court have not yet been jaded, seduced, or disillusioned by a system that works badly and is only interested in locating a defendant and efficiently concluding the case; at times, whether he or she is innocent or guilty does not seem to matter.

Some scholars speak of selective and discretionary justice in relation to court proceedings and these also impact the plea bargaining process because the goal of prosecutors is to get the accused to plead guilty (Rosett 4-5). Justice of this nature is not true justice served. In 1974, President Nixon's National Advisory Commission on Criminal Justice Standards and Goals advised that discretionary interactions in order to convince the accused to tender a guilty plea as well as plea bargaining should be abolished, although Arthur Rosett and Donald R. Cressey insist that this would clog court calendars, despite the fact that The Netherlands, for example, has done just that (162, 165).

James E. Bond, in a massive study, one that cites more than 1,000 cases, complains that plea bargaining "may compromise the integrity of the... system"; it "may lead to inaccurate and unjust convictions"; and other problems (48-49ff). Better would be the abolition of plea bargaining, which would allow for trial by jury as guaranteed by the Constitution, the result of which would be true justice rather than a legal boondoggle. Critics have had little effect, although their condemnations can be severe. For example, Emilo C. Viano, who especially dislikes the fact that the innocent plead guilty, insists that "Negotiated justice as it is currently practiced in the United States produces innumerable miscarriages of justice..." or worse, it is "a perversion of justice." This is certainly a problem: In 2023, "...803 people in the United States since 1989... pled guilty and were later proven innocent" (Fadel). What this strongly implies is that coercive prosecutors suborn the accused to misrepresent the truth, that is, to blatantly lie, and although prosecutors are not allowed to distort the truth, they may occasionally do so. Purposely misleading, lying, deceiving, or duping is generally considered to be unethical in any context. In legal situations it is especially dangerous; indeed, lying under oath (perjury) carries heavy penalties.

Even more horrific is the habit of prosectors to strongly desire to complete a case as swiftly as possible and so they do many unsavory things. Here is an egregious example: "...[P]rosecutors have used threats to indict children, spouses, or other family members to induce pleas of guilty, including in cases where the pleas served to cover up pervasive law enforcement misconduct that would have been revealed at trial (Dervan). Some of these shenanigans are worthy of a Soviet Gulag show trial.

Reforms and Alternatives

Plea bargaining has not raised the hackles of reformers the way that bail bonding has and therefore reform movements are less extensive. Indeed, as Cynthia Alkon explains, "Professionals in the criminal justice system are often not as critical of the process as scholars and instead often see plea bargaining as a practical process through which they can manage their high caseloads. Practitioners, therefore, *often resist efforts to prevent the use of plea bargaining* and find ways to continue plea bargaining cases" (italics added, 2). Quite some time will have to pass before it is mildly improved. Radical alteration may never occur. One reason for this is that this pleading takes place between the accused and a prosecutor. There is no intermediary commercial bail bondsman intercalating himself into the judicial process in order to earn a substantial profit and so there is less incentive to ameliorate conditions (and even in bail bonding things change very slowly). Another reason may be that bargaining is often extremely beneficial to the accused (and the state) and so fewer reformers wish to alter or eliminate a system that has been fully implemented only since the early twentieth century and one that improves the lot of the accused and streamlines the judicial process but does both at the expense of true justice. See the Plea Bargaining Institute (https://pleabargaininginstitute.com/about-pbi/) which provides a forum for discussion and reform of plea bargaining, a system that has grown sporadically and without much regulation so that it varies from one jurisdiction to another (Dervan). What this obviously means is that pleas will be accepted or rejected depending on whether one committed a crime in Chicago or Los Angeles, New York or Atlanta. This is illogical, biased, unfair, and unjust. Even worse is that "As Stafanos [sic] Bibas observed, '…a $100 credit-card purchase of a microwave oven is regulated more carefully than a guilty plea that results in years of imprisonment'" (Alkon citing Bibas, 8). The bottom line, as indicated by the conservative Libertarian Reason Foundation, is that "…plea bargaining is currently overused and abused, often to the detriment of justice" and it therefore requires amelioration especially because of its coercive nature (Mantle). On March 29, 2023, The Federalist Society broadcast "Should We Heed Pleas for Plea Bargaining Reform?" This video is available at (https://www.youtube.com/watch?v=JTUUbB9ylJ8). Two monographic treatments that might help readers are William R. Kelly with Robert Pitman's *Confronting Underground Justice* and Richard L. Lippke's *The Ethics of Plea Bargaining.*

Minor Reforms

Despite the remark above that this travesty is not widely condemned, some folks are aghast: Somil Trivedi of the ACLU entitled his commentary "Coercive Plea Bargaining Has Poisoned the Criminal Justice System. It's Time to Suck the Venom Out." And to prove his point he presents three "heartbreaking"anecdotes, the first of which runs as follows: "In 2006, George Alvarez was charged with assaulting a prison guard while awaiting trial on public intoxication. He knew he didn't do it—the guards actually jumped him—but the ten year mandatory minimum sentence at trial scared him so much that he pled guilty. Little did he know that *the government had a video proving his innocence, but they buried it long enough for prosecutors to extract the plea first.* George spent almost four years behind bars fighting for his innocence before finally being exonerated" (italics added). This speaks for itself.

As early as 1971, Welsh S. White suggests some minor alterations: "Several assistant prosecutors should be given responsibility for negotiating guilty pleas with defense counsel at the earliest possible stage in the proceedings." He seems to think that this would solve many problems (453). Additionally, "To insure effective plea bargaining, the district attorney must maintain some control over the executive prosecutor's exercise of discretion" (457). There is more here but the end result is the same: Pleas will be entered for the wrong reasons, accepted, and justice will still be denied.

Stephanos Bibas thinks that legislative changes would help and also that "Prosecutors can reduce plea agreements to writing, in plain English, and cc clients when they send those agreements to defense lawyers. Prosecutors can also send defendants and their lawyers letters setting forth their understandings of the likely guideline sentences after trial or a plea, as well as of any enhancements that may apply" (167). Here too there is more but these minor alterations do (have done) little to ameliorate a procedure that is inherently flawed and therefore cannot really be fixed.

Bond suggests that plea bargaining can be reformed through "The mass-produced judge trial," a lessening of punishments, sentencing rotation by judges, and the elimination of crimes that do not have victims (47). In 2019, the American Bar Association formed a task force that in 2023 enacted 14 principles. Here follow seven of the most salient:

"Principle 2: Guilty pleas should not result from the use of impermissibly coercive incentives or incentives that overbear the will of the defendant."

"Principle 3: In general, while some difference between the sentence offered prior to trial and the sentence received after trial is permissible, a substantial difference undermines the integrity of the criminal system and reflects a penalty for exercising one's right to trial. This differential, often referred to as the trial penalty, should be eliminated."

"Principle 4: Charges should not be selected or amended with the purpose of creating a sentencing differential, sentencing enhancement, punishment or collateral consequence to induce a defendant to plead guilty or to punish defendants for exercising their rights, including the right to trial."

"Principle 5: The criminal justice system should recognize that plea bargaining induces defendants to plead guilty for various reasons, some of which have little or nothing to do with factual and legal guilt. In the current system, innocent people sometimes plead guilty to crimes they did not commit."

"Principle 7: There should be robust and transparent procedures at the plea phase to ensure that the defendant's plea is knowing and voluntary, free from impermissible coercion, and that the defendant understands the consequences of their decision to plead guilty."

"Principle 8: The use of bail or pretrial detention to induce guilty pleas should be eliminated."

"Principle 14: At every stage of the criminal process, there should be robust oversight by all actors in the criminal system to monitor the plea process for accuracy and integrity, to ensure the system operates consistent with the Principles in this Report, and to promote transparency, accountability, justice, and legitimacy in the criminal system" (Dervan).

The principles are indicative of the problematic nature of plea bargaining, but with few exceptions they advance only minor reforms. These principles attempt to contain and maintain a harmful system—one that should be expunged—through a patchwork of ostensible enhancements. Those who plead guilty are Constitutionally entitled to a trial; those whom they harm should demand that their antagonists be tried for the precise crime involved and not for a lesser indiscretion conceived by an overweening prosecutor.

Not especially useful, common sense additions to the current plea bargaining system include limiting it to minor infractions; limiting the choices that a prosecutor may make; and including judges and defense lawyers in the procedure so that the naive, ill-informed, and frightened accused are not bullied into agreeing to a plea they neither understand nor desire. It would also be helpful if prosecutors were honest and did not do whatever is possible (if unethical and even illegal) to complete the case and move along to the next one.

Major Reforms

The Fadels suggest the following improvements: "...enforcing strong penalties for prosecutors for wrongful convictions, limiting the number of plea deals prosecutors can offer, excluding plea bargains from the conviction rates of prosecutors, [and] having a judge evaluate whether the evidence against someone is strong enough to warrant a plea deal." Well, this is a small step forward, although these recommendations also merely help to maintain the current system.

Alkon contends that pointed reform is not enough: It is also necessary to change "the underlying criminal law": "The possibility of harsh penalties, combined with prosecutors having the discretionary power to charge the same act as a felony or misdemeanor and to add a variety of sentencing enhancements, contribute to what is often a highly coercive atmosphere in plea bargaining" (26-27). Another possibility is to reduce the number of cases that may be bargained. For example, only felonies or only violent acts may so be adjudicated. Or consider the Australian discount system: "The fulcrum upon which this reform should be based is a designated sentencing discount of up to thirty percent for defendants that plead guilty. This should be supplemented by a higher discount (of up to seventy-five percent) for defendants who plead guilty in circumstances where the prosecution's case against them is weak" (Bagaric 28). This would ensure a more equitable sentence by diminishing the prosecutor's extensive power advantage, but in reality it continues to maintain the plea bargaining system, although with a more equitable allocation of the power differential to both parties. This is extremely important because of the threateningly coercive nature of this relationship, where, as indicated, the prosecutor at times does some very unpleasant, indeed, unethical things. James C Scott, who believes that "marginalized groups subtly undermine authority" (Gabriel), would be quite disappointed to discover that misinformed and frightened defendants are quite powerless to counter their prosecutors.

Radical Reforms

As with bail bonding, only Congress can entirely eliminate this detrimental system that allows the guilty (and the innocent) to bargain away justice. Even if a handful of local jurisdictions or states were to eliminate plea bargaining, it would still obtain everywhere else. And as it happens, only Alaska has banned sentencing bargaining, which is not quite the same thing. Elimination must take place at the national level. To merely tinker with reform or alteration will not fully and completely improve the judicial process for those who have committed a crime and deserve some commensurate punishment. It is good and humanely kind to consider criminals' rights and prison conditions, but the law must also care for the victim and the justice that must follow when an egregious or heinous act is committed.

Consider that Judge Frederic Block, in A *Second Chance: A Federal*

Judge Decides Who Deserves It, argues that sentences can (and should) be commuted: "...[S]ometimes a sentence that made sense when it was imposed can look like a bad fit over time. Prisoners grow old or get sick. The laws under which they were sentenced change. Others who committed the same crimes get starkly different prison terms. Doubts arise about guilt. On occasion, everyone agrees that the prisoner has been thoroughly rehabilitated." He votes for judicial discretion and leniency for criminals while ignoring the victims. The 2018 *First Step Act* "overhauled federal sentencing." "A major feature of the law lets prisoners file motions for compassionate release in 'extraordinary and compelling' circumstances" (Liptak)

Radical alteration has occurred but in a local venue and in a delimited manner: "From 1969 to 1973, the Philadelphia District Attorney's office pioneered a policy of complete abolition of plea bargains. The results were mixed. Instead of clogging courts as some legal commentators had predicted, the reform caused Philadelphia's prosecutors and defense attorneys to bargain over whether the defendant would elect a jury trial or a bench trial" (Mantle). It is unreasonable to think that total elimination is, at this time, possible, since such a high percentage of both federal and state cases are plea bargained. This would clog the courts into unmanageable chaos and the accused would have to wait years for their cases to come up. Still, allowing this system to continue unabated is an affront to true justice. One way to improve matters would be to reduce the number of committed crimes by creating a social system that emphasizes financial equity, thus eliminating the incentive to act dishonestly, although there will always be embezzlers, scammers, hackers, and violent people who apparently cannot help themselves.

As indicated above, of all of the procedures and actions criticized in this diatribe, plea bargaining is the single most harmful because it diminishes the justice ultimately handed down. (Bail bonding critics might disagree.) A felony pled to a misdemeanor reduces the potential sentence dramatically. This is extremely unfair to the victim and society, although it is a treasured boon to the accused. Virtually all of the reforms mentioned above miss the point: They merely prolong a system that should be abolished, and court clogging (and the diminution of retribution) are really bad excuses to maintain it.

International Law

In France (an exemplar of the EU, though the procedure will vary in different countries), plea bargaining has existed since 2004, is only employed for minor crimes, and the sentence must be less than one year (Taleb-Karlsson). And so it is quite different from the US system where most serious felonies are bargained. The complicated French procedure will also differ from that employed in the US. Its benefits, however, are similar: It clears the court calendar for more serious cases. But I do think that the negative aspects also obtain even for these minor crimes: The reduced sentence does not necessarily serve justice; rather it is an expedient that allows the government to employ fewer judges and saves taxpayers money. For the French criminal, who may be facing a ten-year sentence, it is a real bargain. How could he or she resist? It should be eliminated here too. In Japan, a new plea bargaining system was mandated in 2016; it allows for a typical plea to reduce charges but only if the person offers evidence in relation to another person's crime (https://www.noandt.com/wp-content/uploads/2019/09/japan_no09.pdf). Sadly, instead of being eliminated, American plea bargaining is spreading to many countries around the world.

Chapter Three: Probation

Definition

Probation is a system that allows a court to release an offender into society so that he or she can live what amounts to a normal life rather than spend time locked up in jail or prison. It is a halfway measure that controls through a variety of actions not all of which are always mandated; these include the use of ankle bracelets, reporting to a probation officer, community service, and promising to avoid travel. Ignoring these, say, by removing a bracelet, can have severe consequences including probation revocation. (There is also unsupervised probation.) Like plea bargaining, it saves the state and thereby taxpayers the cost of incarcerating someone who does not necessarily pose a threat to society, and yet felons can be probated. "Nationwide, on any given day, more people are on probation than in prisons and jails and on parole combined" because of long terms that range from nine months to ca. five years, with an average of about two years ("States"). Thousands of different agencies oversee this activity and many millions of probationers take advantage of this gift ("Probation"). This site, "Probation and Parole," gives access to programs, reports, articles, and other resources on specialized topics such as probation and—females or juveniles or LGBTI or sex offenders or tribal peoples or veterans and so on.

The *Probation Journal* (https://journals.sagepub.com/home/prb) was founded in 1929 and so it has had almost 100 years to provide a forum for global scholarly insights into probation and its improvement. But in the context of *Justice Denied,* it does not offer much that is useful. For example, from 1959 we have "The Probation Officer, His Training and Skill" and from 2024, "'I'm getting out to nothing': A temporal analysis of dominant discourses and practices with residents convicted of child sex offences in probation Approved Premises." These do little to clarify or improve or abolish the probation process, although there are probably some helpful papers among the hundreds published over the years. Nevertheless, probation continues to haunt and misdirect.

For those with questions, Reddit provides a forum at <r/Probation> with almost 40,000 followers, so there are a lot of people on probation who have real-world queries. Naturally, a lawyer could help here, but fellow sufferers will have a different perspective on drinking, testing, medical marijuana, obstruction, and other subtleties. And since various jurisdictions have different rules, states and counties across the country have websites that can help those living there.

In 1990, Joan Petersilla, mentions that intensive supervision programs, which are more restrictive than traditional probation, may not meet the objectives of incarceration (punishment and control). What is surprising is that some hardened criminals believe that they are just as punitive as incarceration, indeed, "more dreaded than prison" (23). And how are offenders with mental disabilities and mental health problems treated within probation services?

Benefits

I imagine that some good has accrued to some probationers, but it is in reality superfluous. If a person is a threat, he or she should be imprisoned. If innocuous and not guilty of an egregious social harm such as an enormous embezzlement or Ponzi scheme, then the offender should be released on his or her own recognizance and allowed to work to repay victims and society. Violent criminals should not be released under probationary laws. Indicating that society does not fully trust the person to behave without strictures is offensive and counter-productive. Either he or she is capable of living an upstanding life or not.

Detriments

Probation is not a deterrent to those who choose to stray once again and provide a danger to the community. It is reminiscent of my assigned duties as a case worker for the New York City Department of Social Services (Welfare). I was to visit clients in their homes and ask to see their rent and utility receipts to make certain that the recipients of this government largesse paid their bills rather than purchasing alcohol, tobacco products, or illicit drugs. Is it not reasonable to conclude that if they had not been paying their bills, they would have been evicted from their electric-less apartments? Never once did I request receipts; instead, I consoled by listening to their stories and commiserated, helping and palliating. And I went out of my way to insist that the stubborn medical social worker allow a phone for a blind woman. It was like pulling teeth, but I prevailed.

As early as 1985 (and presumably much earlier) probation, especially for felons, was problematic and controversial: "The probation debate seems to have reached an impasse." Those in favor of probation claim that it reduces crime, costs, and overcrowding; those who oppose it want harsher sentences, insist that it allows too much "judicial discretion," and it fails to reduce crime. For example, felons probated in Los Angeles and Alameda Counties had a 65% recidivism rate (Petersilla et al. 12, 20).

In *Practice and Theory of Probation and Parole,* a 1959 study, David Dressler presents a detailed overview of the historical development and evolution of each of these procedures. This may be of some interest to those who wish to trace the way that probation and parole have worked over the centuries, but it has little applicability to the ongoing harm that probation and parole continue to cause a quarter of the way through the 21st century. To indicate that a high percentage of released criminals are recidivists does not take into account the pain and emotional harm to victims and their relatives. The 2019 overall US rate is 70% and rises to as high as 83%.

A horrible development is the privatization of probation along with parole and prisons. The companies involved are in the business of earning a profit, not advancing justice nor caring for the lives of these folks and their quest for freedom. Incredibly, probationers, who are already poor or destitute, are now saddled with ongoing costs and fees levied by these companies, whose employees threaten to send non-compliant probationers to jail. If a person does not have any excess funds, it will be impossible to pay these superfluous fees. There are also non-profits that replace governmental agencies.

Finally, "Probation and parole were designed to be an alternative to incarceration so people can pay their debt to society and be redirected back to work without wasting prison space. But instead, these systems create a series of trap doors that lock people back up—not for committing new crimes, but often for things like showing up a few minutes late for an appointment or crossing city lines to pick up their child for school. They've become systems that prepare people for prison, not productivity" ("Why"). These are the major reasons why reform is so necessary.

A different perspective on probation, as practiced in England and Wales, is put forth by Rob Canton and Jane Dominey, who criticize officials: "A familiar explanation is racism, sexism, suggesting that the origin of discrimination is to be found in the views of practitioners and their power to give expression to their prejudicial attitudes. A premise throughout has been that probation is best seen not as a way of reducing the prison population nor as a means of enhancing public safety." Instead, punishment provides the rationale for probation here. And "…Community Service (CS) has always tried to incorporate principles of punishment, rehabilitation, reparation and reintegration." The authors are also cognizant of "probation's work with victims" (abstracts). Countering this is Jill Annison and colleagues' "People First" which indicates that changes in the service in the US might have emphasized control over care, but their analysis shows that "individuals enter the training to work with people, and that they continue to achieve most satisfaction from this" (abstract) and so bigotry seems to be absent here.

Reforms and Alternatives

One possibility, which I do not favor, is community supervision. This is in reality merely a euphemism for probation (or parole). "Wide variations in policies and term lengths across states point to opportunities for reform" because "More than 1 in 10 state prison admissions are the result of technical violations of probation rather than convictions for a new crime" ("States"). Petersilia and her colleagues suggest that probation should be redefined, limited and aim for just deserts, among other possibilities (87, 89). "REFORM focuses on breaking the supervision-to-prison pipeline and seeks to replace it with one that creates clear and fair pathways to work, wellness and stability; that will create safer communities for us all" ("Why"). The Coalition for Juvenile Justice publishes "Probation Reform: A Toolkit for State Advisory Groups" (https://www.juvjustice.org/sites/default/files/resource-files/Probation%20Reform%20Toolkit-2.pdf). Various states such as Virginia, Kentucky, Georgia, Iowa, Arizona, and California have tried to reform this painful process.

Minor Reforms

Because terms are longer than required for public safety, if the length of sentences was reduced, the probation population would shrink, and goals instead of time served, earned time credits, and reviews of probationers would improve matters ("States"). Furthermore, since the state in which probation occurs influences the length of the sentence (in 2018 in Hawaii the average was almost 59 months, in Kansas just over nine), it would, as usual, be beneficial if there were a national standard ("States"). "States should analyze data to determine potential probation reductions and policies" and "Court authority [does exist] to terminate probation early" ("States"). But these minor alterations do not radically change the probation business, which in bureaucratic essence is similar to bail bonding, although here rather than governmental profits, there are only deficits—for personnel salaries and supplementary overhead costs.

Major Reforms

A "New Report" presents four useful recommendations: 1 "Restrict the use of incarceration as a punishment for technical violations of probation and parole." 2 "Replace automatic incarceration for alleged violations with a written notice to appear in court." 3 "Apply earned-time credit to supervision sentences." And 4 "Bolster due process." But these are merely suggestions. In the summer of 2024, a major Delaware bill that would have brought significant changes to the state's probation system failed to pass, though the ACLU really tried (Brickner). And it is hard to believe but "In Pennsylvania, 54% of prison admissions are for supervision violations…." And so it is good that "…a law designed to ease the more draconian provisions of Pennsylvania's probation system…" passed in 2024. This will change a system that allows minor technical infractions to send people back to prison (Tung).

Michelle S. Phelps, emphasizing juveniles, insists that "Community supervision in the United States is uniquely punitive" (131). Reforming the system includes the following: "Increase Real Decriminalization and Diversion in Sentencing" (136), "Improve Supervision for Smaller Caseloads" (137), and "Reduce Revocation Rates and Disparities" (138). Finally, "Reforms that draw on the desistance model improve relationships between probationers and officers by building a more respectful and collaborative dynamic" (138).

Radical Reforms

Nothing could be more radical than the complete abolition of probation, something that criminologists, jurists, laypersons, and criminals would find abhorrent, but its benefits are outweighed by the recidivism of its violent participants and the harm that they do to their victims. In all matters pertaining to the law, I favor the victim over coddling criminals, some of whom are not rehabilitatable. Despite the belief that Waller and his colleagues forward that no one is morally responsible for his or her actions (see the introduction), some human beings are so vile and harmful that they should be permanently incarcerated both as punishment and especially to protect society. Liberal reformers will disagree. Victims (or their relatives) of violent crime (assault, rape, kidnapping, murder) or even those bilked out of their retirement savings will certainly not sympathize with the criminals responsible for their pain.

Brian K. Lovins and his colleagues suggest that the entire corrections system should be reimagined and probation is the main area to be reformed by focusing on rehabilitation; rather than managing failure officers will become coaches who will forward success (abstract).

Here is something that really worked: "Sites participating in deep-end reform minimized probation dispositions for youth with misdemeanor charges and developed meaningful interventions for youth assessed as being at high risk of rearrest." Deep-end reform should improve probation (Esthappan 2). "Though the deep-end approach addressed key decision points throughout the JJ system, most investments were directed toward narrowing the pipeline of referrals to the system, rethinking dispositional decisionmaking, and improving probation practices. Sites implemented numerous changes to policy and practice to minimize judicial dispositions to probation and out-of-home placement by increasing preadjudication diversion, limiting probation recommendations to out-of-home placement, and reducing the use of probation revocations" (Esthappan 3). "The deep-end sites' experiences with probation reform illustrate many hard-earned lessons applicable for other jurisdictions interested in similar reforms. Central to any collective change process is a unified vision for change; a lack of consensus among stakeholders on that vision can hinder progress"

(Esthappan 9). Although this program is aimed at juveniles, it offers much that can influence reform in all jurisdictions.

In 2010, Jeffrey Rosen published "Prisoners of Parole" (in which he discusses probation rather than parole); he explicates a plan (the 2004 HOPE program) implemented by Judge Steven Alm, who was dissatisfied with probationers' constant unpunished petty infractions, so he indicated that offenders would be mildly punished *immediately* for probation offenses. This is a radical departure because it worked incredibly well. Instead of making repeated minor offenses, probationers behaved themselves. The conclusion is that "The HOPE program, if widely adopted as a model for probation and parole reform, could make a surprisingly large contribution to reducing the prison population."

Finally, Mark Kleiman's rather outlandish, utopian plan is discussed by Patrick Kelly and Don Stemen: "Kleiman's plan calls for placing roughly four million people in a reformed probation-like community corrections program. Within this group he would include the one million individuals with the lowest crime rates (weighted for severity) among the more than two million currently behind bars; the two million highest-risk offenders currently under community supervision; and another one million individuals 'who ought to be on probation or parole, but who aren't—that is, the highest-crime group among recently convicted people who aren't under community supervision.' He also envisions a number of changes to the regime that would supervise these four million. The new system would have a small set of rules, each of which would be linked to crime reduction. Any rules that couldn't be effectively monitored would be eliminated. Also, the system would impose swift and certain—but usually mild—sanctions whenever it detects a failure to comply with the rules. Except when there are new crimes or in cases of repeated failure to appear for parole or probation check-ins, Kleiman would eliminate revocation: 'Probation,' he said, 'should not be something you can flunk out of'" (2). Some commentators criticized aspects of the plan (passim).

International Law

According to Martine Herzog-Evans, probation in France has existed since 1946; it has ben reformed but still controls released offenders and those with suspended sentences and aims at rehabilitation. The system is a farrago of older and more recent alterations, the result of which is that the old and new methods make life difficult: Evidence based probation practices are abjured and the staff is under stress. "The future does not look good for French Probation" (345, 349, 351). Japan's probation system is most unusual because it employs volunteers to help professionals, but the goals are the same: to mentor and help rehabilitate. The Volunteer Probation Officers (VPOs) only supervise one or two offenders and the professionals supervise 30 VPOs in this community-based system (Kato, 117, 119, 118).

Chapter Four: Parole

Definition

Parole (provisional or supervised release) is a system employed in some venues to allow a prisoner who has served some of his or her sentence to be released, often for "good behavior," a bizarre locution more appropriately assigned to primary school children who did not cry, brawl, or soil their pants. Parole is so controversial that 17 states have eliminated it. This obviously means that 33 still allow sometimes dangerous criminals to be released into the community and naturally each jurisdiction operates differently with different rules and regulations. What this means is that a person convicted of armed robbery in one state will achieve parole differently than someone convicted elsewhere for the same crime.

The Unites States Parole Commission (USPC) "...promote[s] public safety and strive[s] for justice and fairness in the exercise of its authority to release and revoke offenders under its jurisdiction." At times, scammers claiming to be USPC employees contact people and attempt to collect either data or money or both (https://www.justice.gov/uspc). Federal parole with few exceptions was abolished in 1984 (https://en.wikipedia.org/wiki/Parole) and 17 states have abolished parole. So, parole in various states exists in one bad form or another or it has been expunged. This is why we require a federal policy that obtains in all 50 states. Violent offenders should serve their sentences; others can be released early on their own recognizance with severe penalties for reoffending.

Benefits

Parole has two benefits: It allows a prisoner to be set free and it saves the state and taxpayers millions of dollars, since the yearly cost to house a single person in a federal penitentiary is more than $40,000.

But justice is not served by shortening a sentence especially for those convicted of violent crimes. It would be far superior to give shorter sentences, if parole is to be considered in the future and the judge should take this into account. Sentencing someone to 25 years to life or even 30 years without parole, but knowing that the possibility of parole will come up 15 years down the line, just does not make good sense. Humanitarian parole, which is quite different, may be granted to some immigrants.

Although many thinkers deplore parole, the Restore Justice Foundation advocates for it and cites Illinois' abolishment, which resulted in increased incarceration rates. Parole, it claims, reduces both costs and crime (https://www.restorejustice.org/learn/why-parole-matters/) but it ignores the detriments.

Detriments

As long ago as 1975, Michael Mandel caustically criticized the Canadian parole system and those who lamented its flaws: "Parole has received a lot of attention lately. The usual gaggle of indignant editorialists, angry letter-writers and ambitious backbenchers has been accompanied in the seventies by a virtually ceaseless flow of committee reports, penological investigations, judicial decisions and ministerial announcements. Most of this is interesting and some even illuminating, but it is all disappointing for one basic reason: the failure to subject the entire enterprise to a systematic critical evaluation" (501). He goes on to find fault with economics (it is very expensive) (503); sentence length ("a 9.9 percent reduction in the time spent in prison" but there also may be a lengthening effect) (512); and pains of parole (controls behavior: "Anxiety, fear, loss of dignity, excessively limited freedom, uncertainty of one's future—these are the pains a parole system brings with it…") (521, 523).

Being released from prison would seem to be extremely beneficial but surprisingly there are many sometimes insurmountable problems. One may be stigmatized; the rules that parole bequeaths are at times counter-productive, for example, disallowing one to look for a job while idling time away at the parole office. And locating housing and a job, reconnecting with family, and dealing with health issues can be daunting, (Scott-Hayward 425, 428). All of these factors stymy successful reentry into society.

Parole arrives with stipulations and they are so frequently abrogated that a whole array of parole violations exist. These include failure to report to a parole officer, moving without permission, using drugs, not adhering to a curfew, and rearrest, among other offenses. Criminals sentenced to 15 years to life, life without parole, 150 years, and other severe sentences should not be given early release. This vitiates the judgment and sentence imposed for the specific crime and harms the victim and/or her relatives mentally and emotionally because justice is not fully served. I am well aware that this appears to be especially unjust to those who have fairly served part of their sentence and perhaps do deserve early release, but this system also serves the evil criminal, the recidivist who returns earlier to a life of hurting others. Here is how this works: Norman Mailer, the extremely famous and influential author of a host of books including *The Naked and the Dead,* advocated for the early release of the killer Jack Henry Abbott because he was ostensibly a talented writer. Why this should influence a parole board's decision concerning a murderer is beyond me. At any rate, Abbott was paroled and soon solved a restaurant problem by killing the waiter. After he returned to prison, he committed suicide. This sociopath should have spent his entire life in asocial isolation. Parole in this case was a societal disservice, as it was in the Leopold/Loeb case discussed in the introduction. And my guess is that if Sirhan manages to live to 100, he too will be released upon his 20th application.

There exist many examples of mistaken early release of violent criminals including serial killers. Let me limit these remarks to Leslie Van Houten, a Manson killer who failed many times but eventually was paroled in part because her mentor and advocate described her as "kind, thoughtful and compassionate." This is a miscarriage of justice for the reasons noted above. Surprisingly, Steve Smith concludes his article by indicating that "As of July 11th [2023] Leslie Van Houten is now free and we are all less safe." I do doubt that this woman will commit another crime, so Smith exaggerates here, but she should not be free after participating in an orgy of murderous deaths. Her punishment was justly meted out; she should serve her time.

For those who are sympathetic to Van Houton and other socio- and psychopaths, murderers, and serial killers (instead of their victims), I suggest they consider Leroy Schmitz, who killed his girlfriend but was paroled and then killed his wife (https://missoulian.com/whitefish-murder-suspect-convicted-of-similar-killing-in-massachusetts/article_eb4450ef-0a04-53b5-a7c9-19339b411c52.html); but also see "Paroled Murderers Who Were Freed Only to Kill Again" (https://www.ranker.

com/list/paroled-murderers-who-killed-again/jacob-shelton); as well as "A Short List of Murderers Released to Murder Again (https://www.wesleylowe.com/repoff.html), a compilation of some 80 truly horrifically vile people; among other possibilities.

Many objectors to parole (and other legal boondoggles) care primarily about protecting society, that is, avoiding harm to other potential victims, so their motivation is societal defense (distributive or procedural justice) rather than restorative (making things better), though many may care about this too. A few including this author, as earlier noted, are most interested in retribution, that is, punishment for the harm that the criminal has perpetrated. This is out of favor in our hyper-liberal age, especially when minorities are considered. Anti-retributionists inform us, as mentioned earlier, that a high percentage of prisoners are African American. This is certainly a sad stare of affairs, but it does not logically lead to coddling real criminals by paroling them early. Rosenbaum makes this clear in *Payback,* for which see below.

The Department of Justice's Bureau of Justice Statistics publishes a detailed document that presents a very broad array of data. The 2020 example, "Probation and Parole in the United States, 2020" indicates that there were just under a million people on parole and three million on probation and the latter has been trending downward (https://bjs.ojp.gov/content/pub/pdf/ppus20.pdf). It would be socially beneficial if the trend continued and eventually reached zero.

A not entirely germane counter-argument that critics of retributive justice undoubtedly field is that many innocent people are imprisoned and for long periods of time. This too is unfair, unjust, and vile, and it is often due to the overzealousness of prosecutors who only want to locate and convict a guilty party even if he or she is innocent. And as most folks insist, it is better to allow 100 criminals to go free rather than imprison one innocent person. But the imprisoned innocent do not excuse the imprisoned guilty. The Innocence Project helps to free those who should not be incarcerated. It is unnecessary to waste time feeling sorry for the predators, rapists, and serial killers for whom parole should not be an option. It. is their victims who deserve commiseration. It took years for Connie Francis to overcome the nervous breakdown and trauma of a horrific rape. Should we sympathize with her assailant? And why are the killers of police officers paroled with some frequency? This is an egregious breach of justice.

Finally, it is extremely unpleasant to note, based on reported personal knowledge, but parole officers, like some prison guards, are not nice people and so bad results accrue. This is especially the case when a parolee is belligerent and angry and injures or kills an officer.

Reforms and Alternatives

Parole is beneficial to those who have behaved themselves in jail or prison as well as to the government that thereby saves taxpayers' dollars but it is in dire need of reform or abolition because it is unjust to so expunge part of a sentience and the recidivism rate for released prisoners runs from 13 to 61 percent. Liberal reformers also wish to release more prisoners, especially those who are not guilty of egregious or harmful breaches of the law. The National Parole Transformation Project advocates for change, and reform movements exist in Alabama, Mississippi, and California but sometimes nothing actually improves (https://www.macarthurjustice.org/litigation/national-parole-transformation-project/). This is a shame, since more than 40 percent of released offenders are back in prison within three years (Marchese).

Lilla Gabrieli and her 14 colleagues present a comprehensive overview of various legislated and potential reforms at the state and federal level. These cover "rehabilitative programs in prison, responses to parole violations, making parole boards more objective, and altering the response to parole violations" (42). But none of the reforms are radical in nature.

Minor Reforms

The REFORM Alliance lists a variety of possibilities that could and do improve matters: youth, elder, and medical parole; reasonable sentence lengths; resources that prevent reincarceration; restorative justice; community support centers; job training; and housing support ("Why"). Supporting released offenders in every way will decrease recidivism rates and allow these people to reintegrate into society and live productive and fulfilling lives. But none of this really improves the parole system, which is inherently flawed because it allows criminals to return to society before their sentences have been completed. In the case of an embezzler whose ten-year term is reduced to five so that he can earn a living and repay his victim, this may be a good thing for all concerned. But for a violent abuser or murderer to leave after only ten years of a sentence of 30 years to life without parole is extremely unjust to the victim and society. In New York, improvement has been considered in elderly eligibility and standards especially since racial disparities are so ubiquitous (Williamson). Louisiana. Mississippi, and West Virginia have passed legislation requiring minor improvements (Marchese). "California implemented a system which allows individuals who participate in rehabilitation programs (such as schooling and self-help programs) to earn credits towards reducing their sentences, and thus enables individuals to qualify for parole sooner" (Gabrieli 43). This is beneficial but merely a minor alteration.

Major Reforms

In 2023, the Immigration Parole Reform Act of 2023 was introduced in Congress. "This [House] bill limits the authority of the Department of Homeland Security (DHS) to grant immigration parole (i.e., give official permission for an individual to enter and temporarily remain in the United States)" (https://www.congress.gov/bill/118th-congress/house-bill/2453#:~:text=Introduced%20in%20House%20(03%2F30%2F2023)&text=This%20bill%20limits%20the%20authority,remain%20in%20the%20United%20States).). At the time of this writing, it has not become law and many people would consider this a deterioration rather than an improvement to the parole system.

In a 2024 *New York Times* opinion piece, Barbara Hanson Treen, a former New York State parole commissioner, advocates for the passage of two legislative reform bills that would help worthy candidates of the aging prison population gain their freedom. These older incarcerated are often ill or demented and so Treen sympathizes with their plight. Additionally, it costs 100,000 to 240,000 dollars to house one person 55 or older. Therefore, cost, improbability of future harm, and sympathy for the languishing prisoner inform Treen's lament. But of violent criminals, she admits that "Even the harshest punishment can never undo the incredible harm they caused, but encouraging them to take accountability, to investigate and transform their thinking and behavior and to work toward repairing harm is the truest form of justice." I am not so sure and I wonder how many victims would agree." By passing these bills, the lawmakers would be voting to replace a system of permanent punishment rooted in insatiable vengeance with a system that allows for the possibility of redemption and repair.

They would also save an estimated $522 million per year, according to Columbia University's Center for Justice."

"In a series of recent U.S. Supreme Court cases, the Court has partly relied on adolescent brain science to ban capital punishment for juveniles, ban life without parole for non-homicide juvenile offenders, ban mandatory life without parole for juvenile offenders, and to apply the previous decision retroactively by allowing the resentencing of individuals who faced mandatory life sentences as juvenile offenders" (Gabrieli 50). This is a step forward for parole reformers but a blow to the victims of violent crime who may feel cheated merely because the offender was 17 rather than 18 years old.

Radical Reforms

The Sentencing Reform Act of 1984 disallows parole when a federal crime is involved (https://www.congress.gov/bill/98th-congress/house-bill/5773). This too may be considered a regression rather than a reform. The "New Report" (see probation section) summarizes New York State's implemented Less Is More Act which resulted in the immediate release of 2,000 prisoners, the closing of six stare prisons, and the diminution of "...the state parole population by 40%...." This is certainly a radical and probably positive alteration.

International Law

Parole in France is similar to its counterpart in the US. It is possible to remain in prison but be granted provisional release on a daily basis. In Japan, very few life-time prisoners are paroled. Rehabilitation is the goal. The system has remained unchanged for decades but change is now underway. A reformed "...person may be paroled by a disposition of a government agency after that person has served one-third of the term sentenced or ten years in the case of life imprisonment" (Toda).

Part Two Anomalous Transgressions

There exist hundreds of minor legal infractions, which in and of themselves have few real-world consequences. Using vulgar language with a police officer or driving a clunker with no muffler or lights are hardly worth mentioning unless the offender hits the officer or the car explodes and harms a pedestrian. There are laws that cover such things even if not directly related to the precise offense. No large society can function without some encroachments on its citizens' freedom. Recall that New Hampshire's motto is "Live Free or Die." So an African American covered this slogan on his license plate. A judge ordered him to remove the tape. He was hardly living free!

Some of the activities discussed below are very difficult to defend and I am not advocating for them. I too do not favor incest, prostitution, recreational drug use, or even alcohol consumption. Nevertheless, they are all excellent examples of activities controlled by problematic law and many of them would be dramatically improved if they were decriminalized.

Chapter Five: Crimes without Victims

Definition

Crimes without victims are illegal activities that do no harm.

Benefits

Generally, there are no benefits to victimless crimes. But see below.

Detriments

With all of the horrible criminal activity in the world, much of which really harms a great many victims physically, mentally, emotionally, and financially, it is indeed repugnant that legislators and subsequently police and the courts concern themselves with victimless crimes, almost all of which are merely social taboos somehow becoming state or federal legal strictures because of overzealous, agenda-driven, or religiously-minded legislators. Yes, some of these people are following in the footsteps of their constituents, but others who, for example, were bigoted, helped to pass anti-miscegenation laws, the last of which, incredibly, still obtained in 1967! (Cf. Loving v. Virginia.) Some of these "crimes" are laughable, public nudity, for example, which may be considered a felony, one that carries a long jail sentence.

Incest

Let me begin with a very difficult taboo (not based in genetic harm, something unknown thousands of years ago) which is almost impossible to overcome and this is *incest*, sexual activity with a close relative: sibling, offspring, or parent. In many US states, it is even illegal to marry a first cousin, though it is perfectly acceptable in Europe.

Sexual relations with *consenting* siblings or parents are prohibited even though no harm accrues. And the general public would find such acts reprehensible, even nauseating, but this is merely because of social indoctrination. It certainly should not be against the law, though it too can be a felony with very harsh penalties. Incestuous relations have occurred throughout history, in ancient Egypt and within the Hapsburg dynasty, for example. Those interested in this aspect should see the *Wikipedia* entry at <https://en.wikipedia.org/wiki/Incest>. Just how horrific some societies view incest can be seen in the denouement of *Oedipus Rex,* in which the protagonist discovers that he has killed his father and married his mother. He is distraught and physically lacerates himself. But the taboo makes sense because some fathers harm their young daughters, something that occurs despite the illegality of the act.

Now consider *The Kiss*, Kathryn Harrison's memoir about her sexual relations with her father. Because of our socialized attitude, this is extremely controversial and hard to digest. (Do not confuse incestuous relations between consenting adults with harm to minors, that is, children, which is reprehensible.) Dr. Richard P. Kluft points out that "Few subjects in psychiatry elicit more profound, visceral, and polarized reactions than incest." And further, "The treatment of incest victims is often painful and difficult." This implies that one of those involved was either not an adult or was unwilling to participate. This naturally is an act of violent assault and/or rape, both of which are contemptible and against the law. See *Imagining Incest: Sexton, Plath, Rich, and Olds on Life with Daddy*, Gale Swiontkowski's astonishing critical study featuring four of the twentieth century's most acclaimed

female poets, as well as the video *I went to the Incest Capital of America* for some revelatory remarks (https://www.youtube.com/watch?v=U8EAljABohM).

Polygamy and polyandry are also off limits, even though the former was practiced by early Mormons (and may exist today, although it now contravenes church dogma). Why would a government object to such marriages? This is a religious taboo. Polyamory has managed to avoid legal constraints; in any case, it is none of your business unless you are engaging with other polyamorous lovers.

Reforms and Alternatives

There are no reforms indicated for general victimless crimes, but some of the individual offenses have come in for change or amelioration.

V. Bailey and S. McCabe, in a 1979 article, persuasively argue that incest laws in the United Kingdom should be abolished (abstract), but this is not quite the same thing as actually altering the law there or in the US. On the other hand, those affected by abusive incestuous relations between adults and children are against decriminalization and this makes perfect sense, but harming children is always a crime. In Lawrence v. Texas, it was found that "A Texas law criminalizing consensual, sexual conduct between individuals of the same sex violates the Due Process Clause of the Fourteenth Amendment." This somehow is interpreted to apply to incestuous relations. I am not sure that it does. At one time incest was legal in New Jersey but no longer. True reform is not probable in the near future except to assure that incest continues to be a crime.

Minor Reforms

A Kentucky legislator attempted to make sexual relations with first cousins legal, but this tuned out to be a mistake (https://medium.com/@charismaenigma/how-a-kentucky-lawmaker-almost-legalized-sex-with-first-cousins-b017a356d0e1). Additionally, "Incest abuse survivors are deeply concerned about recent news and advocacy efforts that seek to decriminalize incest so that consenting adult family members can marry (https://www.incestaware.org/post/legal-reform-not-decriminalization-will-ensure-the-safety-of-america-s-children-from-incest-abuse). The concern is an advance for protecting children but does nothing for incest between consenting adults. And "...punitive sanctions should no longer be imposed upon those who engage in [incest]. That does not mean that incest ought to be endorsed or encouraged" (https://philosophicaldisquisitions.blogspot.com/2012/09/should-incest-be-decriminalised-part.html). Like so many other remarks, this is merely opinion and carries little weight with legislators or judges. Finally, "Consensual incest advocates are rooting for an anonymous New York parent who wants to marry their own adult child. Australian Richard Morris, who is pushing to change incest laws in about 60 countries, said he supports the legal push in Manhattan Federal Court and that such behavior between consenting adults 'should not be criminalized'" (https://www.latestlaws.com/international-news/consensual-incest-should-be-decriminalized-us-advocates-say). Most readers will find this unsavory at best but in reality extremely deranged.

Scholars, rather than legislators and jurists, favor reform, but as usual these are merely opinions that barley influence change: "...[A]t least among liberal-minded scholars there is a growing consensus that current prohibitions on consensual adult incest are, if nothing else, ripe for reconsideration." Concerning the law, "For the liberal theorist, the line between consensual and nonconsensual sex typically marks what conduct can be criminalized and what cannot." And so, "The case of adult incest is more problematic. An important prima facie right to choose one's sexual partners is at stake here" (Green).

Major Reforms

Probably none.

Radical Reforms

Probably none

International Law

As is often the case **in France,** the law concerning incest is complex, but basically incest is illegal. Very surprisingly incest is not illegal in Japan.

Prostitution

Additional crimes may also give one pause, but upon reflection, any rational person must admit, that *prostitution* (now euphemistically, sex work), for example, is not harmful. The illegality of this act (which is perfectly acceptable in Holland, Germany, Austria—a Catholic country—Turkey—a Muslim country— India—a Hindu country—and Nevada—a bizarre state) is what results in pimping, robbery, assault, and murder. All of the sordid, sleazy, and harmful aspects of this activity would be mitigated and even expunged if it were legalized. The single exception might be trafficking but this occurs regardless of sex work's legal status. Note that this is not meant to mitigate the horrors of trafficking or child prostitution. But the religious do not want people engaging in sexual activity outside of marriage and so we have draconian laws prohibiting a harmless activity. One day, while wandering in a rather seedy San Francisco neighborhood, I saw a large, official sign that read "Johns Lose Their Cars." How dare a jurisdiction create such an unjust law? It is astonishing that San Franciscans, known for their liberality, put up with this.

Prostitution provides a variety of possibilities*. These include street walkers, whom a client encounters in the street, often by chance. Window workers, in Amsterdam, where one finds its infamous red-light district. Escorts, who may or may not engage in sexual activity; these folks can easily be located in Las Vega or Reno. Brothel employees who may work at a legal establishment in Nevada, Innsbruck, Hamburg, Istanbul, Paris, or Thailand among other locations.

Prostitution is so important, influential, and widespread that, amazingly, there exists a two volume *Encyclopedia of Prostitution and Sex Work.*

Reforms and Alternatives

Justice Denied neither advocates for nor defends prostitution but rather insists that it should be legalized, which would solve most of the problems associated with this kind of work. This seems to have occurred in countries in which the state controls commercial sexual activity. Although many people including some legislators agree with this perspective, a few critics do not. In "Ten Reasons for *Not* Legalizing

Prostitution and a Legal Response to the Demand for Prostitution," Janice G. Raymond is unequivocal in her condemnation. Here follow five of her reasons with only brief rebuttals:

- "Legalization/decriminalization of prostitution is a gift to pimps, traffickers and the sex industry." I think that precisely the antithesis is true. Pimps would disappear and perhaps traffickers as well.
- "Legalization/decriminalization of prostitution increases clandestine, illegal and street prostitution." It would no longer be illegal and workers would not have to hide from the police.
- "Legalization/decriminalization of prostitution does not protect the women in prostitution." If they work in brothels, it would.
- "Legalization/decriminalization of prostitution does not promote women's health." Regular medical check-ups would certainly help.
- "Women in systems of prostitution do not want the sex industry legalized or decriminalized." This is based on workers and sex trafficking in five countries including the Philippines (illegal), Venezuela (legal), and the United States (illegal) (passim) rather than in Holland, Germany, India, and Sweden and so the conclusions are biased.

All in all, Raymond argues cogently and persuasively. I just do not agree that decriminalization and regulation would be counter-productive.

Minor Reforms

"In 2009, Rhode Island signed a bill into law making prostitution a misdemeanor. Prior to this law, between 1980 and 2009, Rhode Island was the only U.S. state where prostitution was decriminalized, as long as it was done indoors." And "In 2020, some elected officials introduced bills to legalize prostitution in the state [New York], but those have not received widespread support" (https://en.wikipedia.org/wiki/Prostitution_in_the_United_States). The Rhode Island law naturally is a minor regression, one that results in more harm than good. The New York *bills* accomplish nothing at all. In 2023, "Vermont lawmakers

[were] working to repeal the state's prostitution laws, decriminalizing adult sex work in the state. Proponents of two measures working through the Statehouse say benefits include increased access to public health and safety" (https://www.wcax.com/2023/03/16/vt-bill-would-decriminalize-sex-work/). This too has gone nowhere.

Major Reforms

The ACLU and Amnesty International both advocate for the decriminalization of sex work (https://www.aclu.org/news/topic/its-time-to-decriminalize-sex-work), (https://www.amnesty.org/en/latest/news/2023/09/united-nations-experts-this-week-said-that-that-full-decriminalization-of-adult-voluntary-sex-work-holds-the-greatest-promise-to-address-the-systemic-discrimination-and-violence-sex-workers-frequently/). They could cite sex work legality in many countries and successful decriminalization movements in New Zealand and Belgium.

Radical Reforms

Prostitution is against the law because of religious fanaticism, intolerance, and social taboo, but Elizabeth Nolan Brown points out that Hawaii, New York, and Vermont have recently attempted to decriminalize this act for both sex workers and their customers. For financial reasons, sexual activity in exchange for payment is perfectly legal in Nevada and has been since at least the early twentieth century—as long as there is no gambling nearby. Not surprisingly, there are ways of circumventing this: In cities such as Las Vegas or Reno, *escort* services are acceptable, but who is to know if the escort earns a bit of extra money in the guest's hotel room? Maine was the first state to decriminalize prostitution, bizarrely, only for the sex worker but mot for the customer. The major harm that prostitution causes is human trafficking and this can be reduced through legalization rather than through anti-trafficking legislation: "U.S. trafficking laws perpetuate the distrust victims have toward law enforcement—criminalizing prostituted people fails to end the cycle of victimization and endemic distrust that prostituted people foster towards the criminal justice system" (Monasky 56). The Swedish system of decriminalizing sex work but not its purchase is perhaps the best alternative.

<u>International Law</u>

Things are complicated in France: Prostitution is now legal but hiring a sex worker is not and this carries a stiff fine for the customer. Someone suggested that this is similar to allowing bakers to display their goods but disallowing their purchase (https://www.cnn.com/2016/04/07/europe/france-prostitution/index.html). In Japan, prostitution is illegal, but since there are no penalties, it flourishes.

Assisted *Suicide*

An extraordinary example of a victimless crime, punishable by imprisonment, is *assisted suicide* (which here is taken as synonymous with medical aid in dying and death with dignity). The real crime here is maintaining a life when the person involved is ill and in extreme pain. Even today only 10 states and Washington DC allow death with dignity, i.e., medical aid in dying. Oregon, in 1997, was the first state to legalize this; Vermont, in 2013, was the fourth to do so. In 2023, Vermont became the first state to allow non-residents to take advantage of its euthanasia law. If Michigan had legalized assisted suicide, Dr Jack Kevorkian would not have been convicted of murder for helping to euthanize a suffering patient in 1999; he spent eight years in prison. With the exception of Canada, New Zealand, parts of Australia, and a few European countries, physician-assisted suicide is illegal.

Those unfamiliar with this procedure may not realize that it has some very specifically rigid requirements:

"A patent must

Be at least 18 year of age or older

Have a terminal illness with a prognosis of six months or less to live

Be capable of making their own health care decisions

Be able to make an informed and voluntary request to their physician

Be able to self-administer the medication" (Vermont Ethics Network).

Furthermore,

"The patient must:

Make two oral requests not less than 15 days apart to the physician who will be writing the prescription. Oral requests may be made in the physician's physical presence or by telemedicine if the physician determines use of telemedicine is clinically appropriate.

Make a written request. The written request must be signed in the presence of two (2) witnesses who are at least 18 years of age and who sign and affirm that the patient appeared to understand the nature of the document and to be free from duress or undue influence at the time the request was signed.

Have a second physician confirm that the patient meets the required qualifying criteria" (Vermont Ethics Network).

It is not a crime to alleviate the pain of those suffering from ALS, MS, Parkinson's, cancer, and other debilitating illnesses. The crime consists in forcing a person to suffer, to torture a person because of outdated religious beliefs. This is not 1321, when Dante completed the *Divine Comedy*, in which we find suicides in the seventh circle of Hell along with murderers and tyrants, among other violent people.

And this is a perfect instance of how states' rights and the variations in their laws cause so much harm: Why should a person in Oregon or Vermont be allowed to die with dignity, whereas assisting a fellow suffering human being in Kansas or Kentucky is a felony punishable by imprisonment and in some cases a large fine?

Proponents cite lack of autonomy as a major reason to legitimate a personal choice to cease to exist. This simple phrase can encompass inability to physically act, eat, drink, move, see, hear, think, relieve pain, and other horrors. No one who can no longer cope with a tortured life should be forced by religious fanaticism and the law to prolong his or her misery. Surprisingly, the disabled disagree: Marilyn Golden and Tyler Zoanni strongly insist that legalization is dangerous: "This article is an overview of the problems with the legalization of assisted suicide as public policy. The disability community's opposition to assisted suicide stems in part from factors that directly impact the disability community as well as all of society. These factors include the secrecy in which assisted suicide operates today, in states where it is legal; the lack of robust oversight and the absence of investigation of abuse; the reality of who uses it; the dangerous potential of legalization to further erode the quality of the U.S. health care system; and its potential for other significant harms. Legalizing assisted suicide would augment real dangers that negate genuine choice and self-determination" (abstract 16). This is a reasonable set of arguments that the disabled might conjure up (and I do not have any intention of disrespecting the disabled) but I also do not think that these criticisms are at all valid. "Fear, bias, and prejudice against" the disabled (17) have nothing to do with an individual's desire to end his or her own life. These well-meaning authors conclude: "As Paul Longmore wrote, 'Given the absence of any real choice, death by assisted suicide becomes not an act of personal autonomy, but an act of desperation. It is fictional freedom; it is phony autonomy'" (27). I just do not think that this is true. (For more details on assisted suicide, see < https://en.wikipedia.org/wiki/Assisted_suicide> and <https://en.wikipedia.org/wiki/Assisted_suicide_in_the_United_States>.)

Reforms and Alternatives

The AMA's Code of Medical Ethics presents diametrically antithetical perspectives on this issue. On the one had, physician-assisted suicide is untenable: "…[P]ermitting physicians to engage in assisted suicide would ultimately cause more harm than good. Physician-assisted suicide is fundamentally incompatible with the physician's role as healer, would be difficult or impossible to control, and would pose serious societal risks." Countering this is the following: "Yet physicians are not defined solely by their profession. They are moral agents in their own right and, like their patients, are informed by and committed to diverse cultural, religious, and philosophical traditions and beliefs. Thus physicians should have considerable latitude to practice in accord with well-considered, deeply held beliefs that are central to their self-identities. In other circumstances, physicians may be able to act (or refrain from acting) in accordance with the dictates of their conscience without violating their professional obligations. Uphold standards of informed consent and inform the patient about all relevant options for treatment, including options to which the physician morally objects (https://code-medical-ethics.ama-assn.org/ethics-opinions/physician-assisted-suicide).

The ethical arguments here are clearcut: On the one hand, one must never take a life; on the other, it is vile to allow someone to suffer and/or lose all personal autonomy. In March of 1997, *The New York Review of Books* published "The Brief of the Amici Curiae" submitted to the Supreme Court in favor of assisted suicide. There is nothing unusual about such a submission. They occur frequently. But the difference here is that its authors include four of the most important and respected twentieth century philosophers: Ronald Dworkin, Thomas Nagel, Robert Nozick, and John Rawls. Rather than concentrating on ethical strictures, "...they ask the Court to recognize that individuals have a constitutionally protected interest in making those grave judgments for themselves, free from the imposition of any religious or philosophical orthodoxy by court or legislature" and "Our Constitution forbids government to impose such [religious or ethical] convictions on its citizens" (4). They conclude: "Each individual has a right to make the 'most intimate and personal choices central to personal dignity and autonomy'" (14).

Failing to allow a person to die with dignity when that is what he or she desires is painfully similar to ignoring Do Not Resuscitate/Do Not Intubate orders, when a patient is unable to speak up and when close relatives, who represent the patient, are ignored. The medical profession should pay attention to the layperson's stated desires. Perhaps if doctors were sued for saving a life, they would be more tolerant of their nonprofessional kin, whose wishes are in line with the oath they take to do no harm. We are harmed when ignored.

Minor Reforms

In 1997, the Supreme Court ruled against assisted suicide in Washington and New York: Washington v. Glucksberg and Vacco v. Quill. This is reformist regression. Reform bills have been introduced in the UK's parliament for almost a century: "Reduced to the essential criteria they employ, the comparative snapshot for the 1936 (first) and 2021 (latest) Bills creates a parallel whereby 'voluntary euthanasia' (1936) became 'assisted dying' (2021), 'fatal and incurable illness involving severe pain' (1936) is now confined to 'terminal illness' (2021), and the need for a 'euthanasia referee' (1936) has been replaced by the 'High Court Judge' (2021) requirement" (Tudosie 155). Sadly, there has been no progress on this front in the UK and assisted suicide is illegal.

There naturally exist innumerable scholarly papers on this topic, but what is astounding is the number of pointed monographs, almost all of which defend assisted suicide.

Major Reforms

Probably none

Radical Reforms

First Oregon altered its law so that death with dignity became a legal recourse for those who required it; other states including Vermont followed, so that now 10 states and Washington DC allow a person to end his or her life with the help of an assisting physician. Some dozen additional states including Maryland and Massachusetts are considering altering their laws.

International Law

France is in the process of legalizing medical aid in dying. Japan has no laws concerning death with dignity. Nevertheless, one can get in trouble for assisting a patient to end his or her life. In Japan, this type of action is illegal.

Abortion

(Disclaimer: This author favors abortion because the government should not be allowed to control our bodies; he simultaneously abhors abortion because it ends the potential life of a child.)

The single most contentious victimless crime is *abortion*. There is no meeting ground here and the arguments on both sides may take place within a single individual, one who is a feminist and insists that women have the right to control their bodies and one who simultaneously cares about life and holds that abortion is murder, a very serious crime indeed. The legal status of abortion has varied dramatically during the course of this author's lifetime. In the 1940s, '50s, and '60s, it was universally illegal in the US, and dangerous illegal abortions resulted in harm and deaths. In 1973, Roe v. Wade legalized it but in 2022, the Supreme Court reversed itself on this issue. Abortion is a victimless crime, if it occurs immediately upon intercourse, but it has a very distinct victim if a woman has an abortion later especially but not only if the fetus is viable outside the womb, which may occur as early as 20 weeks. Recall that joeys are born as tiny, *viable* embryonic fetuses and nevertheless climb up to their mothers' pouches; someone once likened this to a blind man climbing Mt. Everest.

Many organizations and agencies advocate for abortion; they include Planned Parenthood, The National Abortion Federation, The Center for Reproductive Rights, the National Institutes of Health (NIH), and, the World Health Organization (WHO). Others, such as the United States Conference of Catholic Bishops, who are pro-life, fight against abortion. An extraordinary array of books defending abortion exist including *The Fall of Roe: The Rise of a New America* by Elizabeth Dias and Lisa Lerer. On the other hand, see especially Karissa Haugeberg;s *Women Against Abortion* for an overview of attempts to stifle abortion in the US.

Reforms and Alternative

With the overturning of Row v. Wade, abortion is now once again unprotected Constitutionally. There are always individuals who and groups that want to maintain this status but there are also many people who wish to reverse the reversal; therefore, there exist many ongoing reform movements, e.g., Planned Parenthood fights against state bans. Abortion is illegal in some jurisdictions but legal in others, although the status varies from fully accessible (in California and most north eastern states) to restricted (in Ohio) to eliminated (in many southern states such as Mississippi and Alabama).

Minor Reforms

Probably none

Major Reforms

Citizens of individual states attempt to have abortion initiatives on their ballots but these are often blocked by, for example, the governor of Florida. Amnesty International advocates for abortion rights but at times nothing happens: "Through our '1000 Ways to Support Abortion Rights' campaign, we're coming up with creative ways to tell the world that abortion rights are human rights..." and "The reproductive justice movement demands that states address social, economic and political inequalities which prevent people from the most marginalised communities from being able to exercise their sexual and reproductive rights" (https://www.amnesty.org/en/what-we-do/sexual-and-reproductive-rights/abortion-facts/). This Amnesty International site is replete with valuable information that notes the many deaths from illegal abortions but fails to address the downside of later abortions for the unborn.

Radical Reforms

These reforms take two divergent paths. Some wish to completely eliminate abortion, whereas others wish to fully implement it. Both groups strongly advocate for their positions but the law favoring abortion often alters quite slowly if at all. State legislation against abortion has flourished since Row was overturned. Here follow some examples of both perspectives:

California "has pushed through laws to help protect access for providers and patients in other states through shield laws."

Connecticut "passed a series of laws aimed at further protecting the right to an abortion."

Florida's "six-week ban went into effect in May 2024."

Idaho's "current ban went into effect August 2022."

Minnesota "passed several pieces of key legislation in 2023, including bills that repealed a required 24-hour waiting period. Parental consent is also no longer required for minors."

North Carolina's "current ban was enacted by the state and went into effect July 1, 2023."

Oregon "In 2023, the state passed shield laws to protect patients and providers from investigations in other states, and paved the way for those under the age of 15 to be able to consent to an abortion without a guardian" (Crowley).

As one can see from this limited survey, the state disparities are extreme.

International Law

In France abortion is a constitutional right. In Japan, abortion is legal but with certain stipulations.

Statutory Rape

Finally, a victimless crime that may surprise readers is *statutory rape*, which in the distant past set the age of consent at ten! When an adult such as Polanski or the fictional Humbert Humbert of *Lolita* infamy sexually abuses a minor, then statutory rape is a valid accusation and the perpetrator should be severely punished. But when two young 17-year-olds plan to marry and have their parents' approval to cohabit, only a dementedly over-zealous prosecutor would pursue charges. But this is precisely what occurred some years ago. And this exemplifies how statutory rape can be considered a victimless crime. Indeed, today, unlike 75 or 100 years ago, sexual intimacy among minors is ubiquitous. (This should not give the impression that it did not occur with some frequency in the distant past.) Do not confuse statutory rape, which is a legal mechanism, with the many other forms of this repugnant act; these include date, marital, and genocidal rape. The disparity among state prison sentences for this crime is truly astonishing, since it ranges from six months to life!

The legal reasoning in defense of statutory rape is sometimes convoluted. Here is a statement from Sherry F. Colb, a Rutgers University law professor: "What permits legislatures the discretion to enact such laws, ultimately, is the fact that (like drug possession), consensual sex with minors is not a constitutionally protected activity. Even if it is victimless, sex with a minor may be criminalized and punished severely without resort to a force requirement. Indeed, it once was punished routinely in this way, because of misogynist concerns about preserving female purity. In modern times, though, when consensual sex among teenagers is generally understood to be both common and profoundly different from the crime of rape, there might still be a role for statutory rape laws in protecting young girls from actual rapists, through deterrence and through the real possibility of retribution." This is very difficult to accept, digest, and sanction.

Reforms and Alternatives

Legislators and prosecutors will generally not be sympathetic to reforming statutory rape laws, but change does occur especially to rape laws generally. When over-zealous prosecutors cite those who are guiltless except in the eyes of the law (ignoring the spirit of the law), reform is mandated but all alterations are not necessarily positive.

Minor Reforms

"...Stephen Kershnar argues that age-different sex should not be a crime. The argument is that if an activity fails one or more parts of a three-part test then it should not be a crime and that age-different sex fails one or more parts. Specifically, he argues that such sex does not infringe on the minor's right, we do not know whether the sex passes a cost-benefit analysis, and criminalization fails intermediate scrutiny. Perhaps this is unsurprising. States are increasingly recognizing the right of teenagers 16 and older to have sex with one another without criminal penalty and there does not seem to be a significant moral difference between a 16-year-old having sex with a peer and with an adult" (Kershnar, abstract). This, of course, is, for the most part, merely suggestive. Change must take place legislatively.

Michelle Goodwin takes a different tack: "This Article is about reforming the way scholars, legislators, prosecutors, and judges think about this legal process and its means and ends. For example, statutory rape cannot be properly contextualized or understood by focusing exclusively on the plain language (or meaning) of statutes 'that focus attention solely on goals and values'" (487). She condemns the law: "Statutory rape law [produces] perverse outcomes and legal fictions" (488). And Ultimately, "So why should we care that children have sex? On the one hand we care too much—so much so that the criminal law is the central form of regulating teen sex. This form of regulation is derived from statutes that treat all sexual behavior alike, even though consent and context may drastically vary. This Article articulates why the criminal law approach, filtered through the judiciary, leads to absurd results. These absurd results include the extralegal punishments inflicted on youth who are punished for participating in consensual sexual activity, such as lifelong registration as a sex offender. This Article argues that such outcomes are untenable because they are morally wrong and foster harms across a series of areas, including creating social status harms, by reifying racial stereotypes. The criminal law approach also leads to cruel and unusual punishments in an era where sex offender registries are increasingly the norm and a condition of release from prison. Such punishments are disproportionate and unjustified" (540). Her reasons for "an alternative approach" are "Sex between consenting teenagers should not be considered a crime on moral grounds" (530), harsh punishment, and economic expense (531). The alternatives are to implement an economic model to alter youth sexual behavior, that is, to pay them to behave (536) and alternative courts (537). I am skeptical concerning both of these solutions to an inflexible hormonal drive especially when consummated between consensual teenagers.

Major Reforms

Many states have revised their statutory rape laws and the "… Supreme Court has recently struck down gender-based State laws that embody some aspects of sex-role stereotypes in 'Orr v. Orr' (1979)…" because these abrogate the Fourteenth Amendment. "It is suggested that a sensible alternative to traditional statutory rape law would be a gender-neutral statute with a conclusive presumption of incapacity that coincides with the approximate onset of puberty" (Eidson, abstract). I am not certain that this really constitutes an advance. But "[a]s of August 2000, all fifty states have gender-neutral statutory rape laws, in which either a male or female may be prosecuted for engaging in sexual activity with a male or female (who is not the perpetrator's spouse) under the age of consent" (Cocca). This too is a regression rather than an advance.

Radical Reforms

Taking Wisconsin as an exemplar of much that is bad in these laws, its legislation is "ineffective and irrational": "Wisconsin should reform its laws, refocusing upon protecting children from sexual exploitation and allow the regulation of consensual peer relationships to be a matter for individual parents, rather than government" (Olszewski 700, 719). Additionally, "The Ohio Supreme Court in a unanimous decision on June 8, 2011 struck down the state's statutory rape law in a case involving two boys under the age of 13" ("Statutory Rape Between"). Finally, "Many jurisdictions have passed so-called 'Romeo and Juliet laws' which serve to reduce or eliminate the penalty of the crime in cases where the couple's age difference is minor and the sexual contact would not have been rape if both partners were legally able to give consent" ("Statutory"). These laws now protect consenting minors and adults from prosecution. Note that the age of consent in states now varies from 16 to 18 but it is no longer ten or twelve!

International Law

French law stipulates that sex with anyone under the age of 15 is considered rape, with some few exceptions. In Japan, statutory rape is illegal: "The law… criminalizes custodial rape of a minor younger than age 18. The penalty for statutory rape is a sentence of not less than five years' imprisonment with mandatory labor" (https://www.state.gov/reports/2022-country-reports-on-human-rights-practices/japan#:~:text=The%20law%20also%20criminalizes%20custodial,years'%20imprisonment%20with%20mandatory%20labor.).

Other offenses (vagrancy and homelessness, gay marriage, gender transition) briefly noted below in this victimless crimes chapter are not covered under Reforms and alternatives and international law.

Vagrancy and Homelessness

In certain jurisdictions *vagrancy* and *homelessness* are crimes. The former is victimless and should be so treated. The latter may at first appear to be a victimless crime, but a number of caveats obtain here. First, when hordes of people gather permanently in a single urban location, it is indeed harmful to the community esthetically, hygienically, financially, and humanly. Some 25 years ago, I was stunned to see an enormous encampment of homeless folks under the lee of the golden dome of San Francisco's city hall. Homelessness is now a ubiquitous problem and embarrassment: No one should be homeless in the world's richest country. Those who refuse to accept shelter provided by a governmental jurisdiction cannot be forced into an apartment in a democracy, but this also does not mean that he or she may set up a tent on the sidewalk in front of Rizzoli's bookstore on New York's Broadway. Ironically, as I write, the Supreme Court is about to approve homeless encampment bans.

Gay Marriage

Another controversial subject, one that still roils folks, is *gay marriage*. No one is harmed if two men or two women join in a civil union or marriage but even today, the fervently religious object based on biblical injunction, and so it was illegal in many venues as late as 2015, when the Supreme Court ruled in its favor. To understand the full extent of the animosity that this issue raises, consider that Dr Norman Kansfield, an influential official of the Reformed Church, was defrocked in 2005 for officiating at his daughter's wedding to another woman (Traub).

Gender Transition

Even more problematic is *gender transition* and this has not been settled yet. No one is harmed if an adult wishes to assume the gender of a different sex or hormonally or surgically alter his or her body. But this is an insurmountable problem for minors especially very young children who wish to begin medical procedures and have their parents' permission to do so. It is highly improbable that a five or even a ten-year-old truly understands the implications of such seriously radical transformation. And so for minors, a very distinct harm is possible. For adults, this is a victimless crime, but states are, nevertheless, still giving folks a hard time. And reasonably, many states have made it illegal to offer gender affirming care to youngsters. Furthermore, in August 2024, "The Supreme Court… temporarily continued to block Education Department rules intended to protect transgender students from discrimination based on their gender identity in several Republican states that had mounted challenges." And so, "'It is disappointing that the Supreme Court has allowed far-right forces to stop the implementation of critical civil rights protections for youth,' said Cathryn Oakley, the senior director of legal policy for the Human Rights Campaign" (VanSickle and Shear). This is a perspectival problem that may never be settled.

Some commentators include other possibilities such as drunkenness in public, trespassing, and gambling. These *may be* victimless, but it is also quite possible that these activities can cause harm to the perpetrator or actor or a victim. For example, a drunk may break a large storefront window, which occurred when I lived in Reykjavik; or a trespasser could accidentally step into a trap set for weasels and harm himself or he could hunt or fish when the owner disallows this; or finally, a gambler could lose a great deal of money, which would detrimentally affect him and his family. The bottom line, however, is that victimless crimes should not be against the law!

Note: Coincidentally, this author has encountered all of these sex workers or their environments in many countries, (the US [New York, Nevada], Holland, Germany, Turkey), although he has never exchanged monetary payment for sex, that is, he has never had anything to do with a prostitute. Like many people, he finds this distasteful but not everyone agrees: At least four of his friends have visited brothels in Austria, Turkey, Thailand, and the US (and he was a present but non-participating attendant in three of these cases).

Chapter Six: Recreational Drug Use

Definition

Recreational drug usage is a two-edged sword. On the one hand, those foolish enough to want to harm themselves by ingesting opium or opioids, cocaine or crack do so whether it is illegal or not and despite the sometimes extremely harsh consequences or penalties. Legal addictive substances such as coffee, tobacco, alcohol, and now marijuana in many states are responsible for illness or death of users and harm and death to automobile accident victims. No one seems to care except Mothers Against Drunk Driving (MADD) and this group has not altered drinking patterns and driving under the influence among adults and especially young men and also, surprisingly, females. Amazingly, the current cases with which I am intimately familiar concern younger women. During my wild youth in Manhattan, I do not recall a single case of a friend or acquaintance driving while under the influence of any substance, although I knew some youngsters who used drugs the way a horse gobbles up sugar cubes. The illegal status of these substances plays only a minimal role in controlling consumption.

Benefits

No real benefits accrue to those who snort cocaine or inject heroin. They may think that feeling high is beneficial but it is no more useful to anyone including the user than alcohol is to the university student whom I overheard opining that he would "go downtown and drink 'til I puke." Did he mature into a socially competent citizen? It is doubtful: By the time one is 20 or so, one's being and moral compass have had lots of time to develop. Still, I have known cases of youngsters who drank until they were complexly overcome but who later earned advanced degrees and many millions of dollars. So who can say with certitude!

Detriments

Perhaps if drugs had been legalized (but maybe not), a hoard of well-known celebrities would still be alive including Frankie Lymon, who died at 25 because he overdosed on heroin; John Belushi, who was killed at 33 by an injection of a speedball given to him by a groupie/dealer; Amy Winehouse, 27, alcohol (which is legal!); Jean-Michel Basquiat, 27, heroin; and many, many hundreds of others (see https://en.wikipedia.org/wiki/List_of_deaths_from_drug_overdose_and_intoxication).

On the other hand, the argument runs, if all substances were legal, then more people and even minors would become addicts. This is almost definitely false. There might be a slight increase in usage but not every relative, friend, and grandparent would spend his or evenings in an opium den. And when they did, the British Empire did not collapse. Just as prohibition did not work (and if it had, we would be a much healthier country), just so does recreational drug control fail. And it does so at a horrendous cost. The cultivation and manufacturing of drugs in Afghanistan and Mexico, the cartels and drug wars, the violence and deaths, the smuggling and distribution in the US and western Europe, the arrests and incarcerations, the insanely high cost for users, and the inability of the government to tax usage, all militate against illegal status. Virtually everything would improve if these drugs were controlled by the government just as tobacco and alcohol are.

Or so it would seem. Oregon legalized drug usage and things did not go well, which does not mean that legalization would be a universal failure. This is such a pressing problem that something should be attempted (just as alterations are necessary in private armaments' control, for which see below). In a January 2024 editorial opinion piece, *The Wall Street Journal* informed readers that Oregon was rethinking its drug decriminalization policy because overdose deaths had increased dramatically ("Oregon"). This is a sad result but no mention is made of the ongoing criminal processes of producing, distributing, and selling these drugs, which are still illegal elsewhere. It is important to realize that 24 states have legalized marijuana and a 2024 *JAMA* study from 2011 to 2021 of 900,000 adolescents found that usage was lower in states in which it is legal (Richtel). By the way, recreational drug use is a victimless crime, if no one is hurt. But if one is harmed, addicted. or killed because of drug distribution or consumption, then the dealer or user is definitely a victim of his or her own improvident action.

Major social detriments include cartels and drug wars, murder of innocent people, smuggling and distribution in the US and western Europe, high cost for the products (which results in crime in order to acquire the money to purchase the drugs), death from overdoses and contaminated drugs, and loss of tax revenue. Given enough time, things will change, although they may always remain problematic because people are often very foolish, willing to risk their lives to briefly feel "good"; those addicted no longer have a choice. Usage is especially harmful to pregnant women whose infants may arrive addicted. A pregnant friend was so dependent on tobacco that in order to control her smoking, she gave her packs to my wife (who lived below), and from whom she would occasionally demand a single cigarette. I know a person who gets ill if she does not drink coffee in the morning. One can be addicted to many legal substances.

Reforms and Alternatives

Stuart Taylor and his colleagues have a number of valuable insights to offer, although they come from a British perspective: "Policies of drug decriminalisation, legalisation and regulation are materialising in a number of jurisdictions around the world, a phenomena welcomed by critics of prohibition who have long exposed its lack of evidence base…, efficacy…, and legitimacy…. Whilst a number of these reforms have been posited as 'progressive…,' this paper argues that they represent the 'metamorphosis of prohibition' whereby the face of drug policy changes yet the fundamental principles remain unaffected. Inadvertently, this reform 'revolution', camouflages the underlying contradictions that have lain at the heart of global drug policy since they were enshrined in the United Nations (UN) Single Convention on Narcotic Drugs in 1961" (2). They indicate some fallacies including "Prohibiting drugs protects society." "Drug use causes crime and social problems." And "Continued drug use inevitably leads to addiction" (passim). Finally, "The current raft of reforms fail to expose and challenge the very principles that underpin prohibition; instead they perpetuate the flawed discourse upholding it. The drug apartheid is a deeply divisive and damaging system that cannot be adapted, but must be dismantled. Abolition inevitably requires a process of transition, it could begin with the decriminalisation of all possession, cultivation and production for personal use..." (23).

Opinions are opined, suggestions are offered, bills are introduced, but change is elusive. The only inroads against a draconian war on drugs that has failed concerns cannabis and its legalization in 24 states (despite an antithetical federal mandate); this has not seemed to have had a detrimental social effect.

But wait: It was "...decided that marijuana belonged in a category of substances deemed most prone to abuse and of no proven medical value. Over five decades, that designation has led to millions of arrests, which disproportionately affected Black people and hobbled efforts to rigorously study the therapeutic potential of cannabis." But it has recently been revealed, in an unlikely turn of events, that Richard Nixon, who launched the War on Drugs, had said that marihuana is not especially dangerous (Londoño). Had this been known, the many people who suffered because of marijuana's criminalization would have avoided prison.

Minor Reforms

There are not many. In 2013, Peter Reuter asked "Why Has US Drug Policy Changed So Little over 30 Years? "And then spends 67 pages answering his titular query: "popular attitude," "general policy inertia," and "timidity of politicians" (51-52) are his reasons. Only the rhetoric has changed. "It is difficult to write about drug policy in the United States without becoming convinced that much of what is done in the name of reducing human suffering from drug addiction and its consequences is misguided and causes more harm than it alleviates, and also being convinced that the prospects of change continue to be slight" (46). He concludes: "The proposition that policy can do little to influence prevalence of use may seem nihilistic. Far from it. We know that bad policy choices can make drug use, drug distribution, and production more harmful. All that policy changes can in fact do is to reduce the harmfulness of these activities. I believe that this proposition has enormously liberating effects for policy. At present, many laws and interventions are justified because they might reduce drug use, even though we know with greater confidence that they cause harms. If prevalence of use is no longer seen as a plausible policy goal, then the harms can be avoided. Finding a way of making this persuasive to the public is the difficult task" (54). We are not making much progress here.

Major Reforms

Decriminalization and legalization would solve many problems including racial injustice and physical harms, but very little has changed. See Steve Rolles's *Legalizing Drugs: The Key to Ending the War,* which has failed in the same way that prohibition failed. The alterations remain suggestions.

Radical Reforms

The National Association of Criminal Defense Lawyers, among many organizations, advocates for reform: "NACDL calls upon the federal and state governments to end the War on Drugs by declaring all drug use to be a health rather than a criminal problem and immediately repeal all laws criminalizing the possession, use and delivery of controlled substances. NACDL fights the discriminatory enforcement and disproportionate impact of drug laws on marginalized communities." And this is what has occurred: "As of October 2023, thirty-one states and Washington D.C. have decriminalized simple possession of marijuana. Thirty-eight states and Washington, D.C. have legalized medical marijuana, and twenty-two states and Washington, D.C. have legalized recreational marijuana for adults" ("Drug Law"). Alteration has been most successful in legalizing the use of cannabis. More radical changes should follow, since the war on drugs has failed dismally. Be aware that countries such as Iran and the Philippines have murdered thousands of their citizens for drug related crimes. The worst incident I can recall concerns two Australians who were executed in Malaysia for drug crimes, despite the pleas of many countries' statesmen. This is even more reprehensible than the draconian Texas laws of the 1960s that imprisoned people for long periods of time for possessing a bit of marijuana.

Amnesty International also advocates for reform: "Criminalizing drugs does not decrease their use or supply. Instead, it drives the trade underground, increases the harms of using drugs and fuels organized crime, corruption and violence." And so "...the evidence available so far shows that decriminalizing the use, possession and cultivation of drugs for personal use, if combined with an expansion of health and social services, does not lead to higher rates of use. Instead, countries where drugs have been decriminalized have seen a beneficial impact on public health, public security and human rights" ("Drug Policy"). And even the ACLU fights for reform.

In a paper published in 2023, Joshua S. Siegel and his three colleagues discuss attempted legal reforms for psychedelics: "We find that 25 states have considered 74 bills (69 legislative initiatives, 5 ballot measures), with 10 bills were enacted, and 32 are still active. The number of psychedelic reform bills introduced during each calendar year has increased steadily from 5 (2019), 6 (2020), to 27 (2021), to 36 (2022). Nearly all specify psilocybin (67), and many also include MDMA (27). While bills varied in their framework, a majority (43) propose decriminalization, of which few delineate medical oversight (23%) or training/licensure requirements (35%). Generally, bills contained far less regulatory guidance than the enacted Oregon Measure 109. While early legislative efforts occurred in liberal states, this relationship may be shifting over time, indicating that psychedelic drug reform is becoming a bipartisan issue. Finally, an analytic model based on marijuana legalization projects that a majority of states will legalize psychedelics by 2033–2037" (abstract). Although much of the scholarly literature and actual alterations concern marijuana usage rather than serious narcotics such as opioids or heroin, here psychedelics are the reform objective.

A group of authors recommend the following radical implementations which naturally are merely suggestions: "(1) de jure decriminalization of all psychoactive substances currently deemed illicit for personal use or possession (so-called 'recreational' drugs), accompanied by harm reduction policies and initiatives akin to the Portugal model; (2) expunging criminal convictions for nonviolent offenses pertaining to the use or possession of small quantities of such drugs (and releasing those serving time for these offenses), while delivering retroactive ameliorative relief; (3) the ultimate legalization and careful regulation of currently illicit drugs; and (4) the delivery of a new 'Marshall Plan' focused on community-building initiatives, expanded harm reduction programs, and social and health care support efforts" (Lewis W10).

International Law

Recreational drugs are prohibited in France, which may not inhibit their use. In Japan, the laws against drugs are very severe; it is even illegal to employ stimulants.

Chapter Seven: Blue Laws

Definition

Blue laws (Sunday closing laws, day of rest laws) control various things such as the purchase of alcoholic beverages on Sundays. They are not as pressing today as they were in the past but they still do obtain in some jurisdictions and inconvenience or even harm citizens. They result from religious intolerance, puritanical attitudes, and compliant legislators who may or may not agree that stores should not be allowed to sell beer after two am. Here are two truly insane procedures that existed at least as late as the 1980s. After hours and on Sundays, were one to visit an Oklahoma supermarket, she would discover that the open refrigerator cases filled with beer are covered with large sheets of canvas. This 3.2 beer, typical in Oklahoma, rather than five or 12 or 40 or even 65 percent more prevalent elsewhere, is so ineffective that a friend visited accompanied by an enormous cooler, which he set down beside him and proceeded to drink beer after beer; he might have exploded had the bathroom not been handy. Do not get into a huff: Oklahoma is a strange place where chicken fried steak is a delicacy. A more bizarre manifestation of puritanical madness is the illegality of liquor by the drink. Here is how this worked in Oklahoma: Restaurants were not allowed to sell alcoholic drinks, so the guest brought her own bottle of champaign or Bud light and a waiter or waitress came along and poured it for her. This is not all there was: If the server failed to pour the liquid, she and the restaurant owner could have gone to jail.

This was the situation in the early 1980s and things have improved over the last half century, but there are still 33 dry states, that is, counties or towns within these states that restrict or prohibit alcoholic sales. Additionally, blue laws still obtain in many places: "Public selling of commodities other than necessary foods and drinks, medicine, ice, and surgical and burial equipment, and other necessities can legally be prohibited on Sunday. In Oklahoma, a fine not to exceed twenty-five dollars may be imposed on individuals for each offense."

The astonishing extent of blue laws can be enjoyed at "Blue Laws in the Unites States" (https://en.wikipedia.org/wiki/Blue_laws_in_the_United_States#:~:text=11%3A00%20a.m.-,Oklahoma,are%20also%20closed%20on%20Sundays). Massachusetts was notorious for its blue laws that also controlled when various business could be open; these laws have obtained for more than 400 years and some have not been repealed, although they are no longer enforced. States that control purchasing cars, for example, include Colorado, Illinois, Indiana, Iowa, Maine. Minnesota, New Jersey, and North Dakota (https://en.wikipedia.org/wiki/Blue_law#:~:text=In%20Colorado%2C%20Illinois%2C%20Indiana%2C,or%20traded%20on%20a%20Sunday.). In the early twentieth century in Ontario, labor, business, games, sports, gambling, hunting, and bathing, among other activities, were banned on Sundays.

Benefits

Blue laws are as oppressive as the requirement in some Muslim countries that a women must be sheathed in hijabs and other garments. They limit one's freedom and do nothing socially positive. They stop people from purchasing lots of products especially alcohol, but this does not really affect the consumption of liquor, since it can be acquired elsewhere or at other times. If these laws were ubiquitous, then people would stop drinking (although this did not work during prohibition) and they would be much healthier and horrendous automobile accidents that occur because of drunk driving would be eliminated. I do doubt that blue laws have ever really had a positive effect. The Supreme Court affirms these laws despite their religious affiliation. Some claim it stimulates a day of rest.

Detriments

These strictures, which derive from religious fervor, are unconstitutional, as the Supreme Court ruled, but it nevertheless upheld them. They limit our freedom and do little to control purchasing or drinking. They have allowed Sundays to stand out as a religious "day of rest,"even though Seventh Day Adventists and Jews celebrate the Sabbath on Saturday. Where these laws obtain, it is often illegal to race horses or sell automobiles on Sunday, both of which are hardships for racing aficionados and those who may desperately need a new car.

Blue laws infringe our right to act. The laws vary dramatically from state to state with four disallowing the purchase of any alcohol in supermarkets on Sundays to 20 allowing the sale of beer, wine and liquor. For a replete overview see David N. Laband's *Blue Laws: The History, Economics, and Politics of Sunday-Closing Laws.*

Reforms and Alternatives

Instead of reforming or abolishing these statutes (even though they are sometimes ignored), some states are affirming them: In 1970, the Vermont Supreme Court, in a unanimous decision, upheld the states' Blue Laws which ban non-essential sales (https://www.nytimes.com/1970/08/02/archives/sunday-blue-law-upheld-in-vermont.html#:~:text=1%20(AP)%E2%80%94The%20Vermont,Giant%20Discount%20Store%20of%20St.). This was extremely regressive.

Minor Reforms

I have been informed that in South Carolina, at least in the past, Blue Laws controlling alcohol consumption in bars were circumvented by turning the bar into a private club (personal communication).

Major Reforms

Probably none

Radical Reforms

Maine reaffirmed its Blue Laws but most states have eliminated them. Some folks (integralists and Calvinists, for example) would like to revive them. This, naturally, is religiously motivated: "A renewed commitment to serious Sabbath observance by churches and by Christians will, if sustained, have social and potentially social implications" (Tooley). Indeed: The religious will control those who have very different ideas concerning working, drinking, and buying automobiles.

International Law

"Three areas of Paris ban purchase of alcohol after 5pm" (https://www.thelocal.fr/20230525/three-areas-of-paris-ban-purchase-of-alcohol-after-5pm). "The name Napoleon may not be given to a pig. Seventy percent of the music radio stations play between 8:00am and 8:00pm must be by French artists. It is illegal to sell a doll which does not have a human face" (https://discover.hubpages.com/education/Blue-Laws-around-the-World). Well, these are just foolish. The Japanese do not have Blue Laws but they do regulate alcohol production and consumption.

Chapter Eight: Gun Legislation

(Disclaimer: As with abortion, this author is conflicted: He holds that we have the right to own armaments to protect ourselves but simultaneously, he despises the use of guns to harm and kill.)

Definition

Gun legislation concerns the laws that control private gun ownership, all of which ultimately derive from the Second Amendment. This is the only concept covered in this study that should be increased rather than decreased or abolished. Regulation varies dramatically from state to state. About one third of US adults own a gun and most for personal protection; 61% of us insist that it is far too easy to acquire a gun legally; 58% want more effective laws; and only half if us think that gun violence is a real problem (Schaeffer). This latter opinion is bizarre and one would think that if the other folks faced a gun crisis, they might alter their opinions.

Many large stores (Walmart, Dick's Sporting Goods), smaller sometimes inconspicuous shops, online entrepreneurs, and dealers offer armaments for sale. Even today, it is at times far too easy to acquire a gun. Some organizations (the NRA) favor firearms and others, such as Mayors Against Illegal Guns, oppose them. Most people purchase and own guns in order to hunt or protect themselves. A few use these devices to perpetrate illegal acts such as armed robbery or serial killing. A small group of people collect armaments in the same way that children collect dolls or stamps or coins; there are even gun collecting clubs. Rare models sell for thousands and even millions of dollars. A friend sold 20 guns for 20,000 dollars and his wife still owns an old Winchester valued at $12,500.

Benefits

The varying state and federal laws regulating the ownership of guns would be beneficial if they truly controlled who and why individuals (not militias) could purchase and own guns. But influenced and controlled by the NRA, they do not do a very good job. And so lots of people own lots of handguns and, illegally, automatic weapons. Hunting and personal protection are ostensible benefits to gun ownership.

Detriments

The major detriment to private gun ownership is death: the unnecessary loss of life brought on by normal people who lose their tempers, angry neighbors and spouses who plan to murder, and socio- and psychopathic serial killers and assassins. The US and the world generally, at least to some extent, are overwhelmed with weapons and armaments. Some of these "weapons of mass destruction" belong to national governments. This phrase implies very specific entities such as nuclear bombs but it really should encompass lots of other horrendous devices manufactured to kill: flame throwers, machine guns, torpedos, cluster bombs, land mines—all of which can wreak mass havoc. Somehow, in some lands, it is possible for the average citizen to acquire military grade armaments: automatic rifles that fire hundreds of rounds, hand grenades, and even items such as howitzers and mortars. The result, especially in the US, is an ongoing rash of unnecessary deaths, often brought on by young, disenchanted children who pick up their parents' uncloseted weapons (which should be locked in an impregnable gun safe) and head off to school or the mall, where bad things occur.

This is possible because the founding fathers decided that militias were necessary and therefore citizens could legally own weaponry, which at that time were almost inconsequential: Muzzle loading guns fired a single shot, not hundreds of rounds a minute. There were no automatic weapons, fighter jets, carriers, nor submarines. Instead of thinking things through, our self-serving legislators are in thrall to the NRA, with its paltry five million members, some of whom are merely hunters, not psychotic survivalists, and which controls the destiny of more than 333 million people, only a little more than a third of whom own guns. And so these elected officials vote against gun control claiming that the Constitution protects ownership but failing to mention the militias, which no longer exist. The military branches of the government, the national guard, and the reserves are all we need to protect us from a British invasion. What we desperately require is legislation to control the ongoing murders of hundreds of children and adults.

In addition to pusillanimous legislators, the main problem here is the disjunction between the 50 states (and their divergent laws) on the one hand and the federal government on the other. Almost three quarters of a century ago, it was (and still may be) illegal to own an unpermitted handgun in New York State. I recall that we were informed that contravening the Sullivan Act carried a mandatory one year prison sentence. But at the time (and even today), one could easily purchase a handgun in Vermont and friends did so and brought them back to New York City, where they resided in handy hiding places. Were a child to find one (I once did) disaster would soon follow. Additionally, I have heard stories of travelers legally packing handguns in their stowed luggage, emerging from the Kennedy or LaGuardia airport baggage pickup area, and being arrested.

The past does not support the current situation. On historical evidence, Jack Rakove insists that "...the justices are very poor and tendentious historians." These sophisticated and knowledgeable but prejudicial Supreme Court justices refuse to admit that Constitutional allowance does not include military style weapons and, additionally, the Court is wrong that weapons were originally allowed for personal protection; the Second Amendment makes this clear by citing militias.

Gun manufacturing companies continue to spew out hand guns, shot guns, rifles, but also automatic weapons of mass destruction for private purchase. This is how individuals acquire AK47 automatic weapons, although they are often illegal. The owners store them in the garage, shop, or hall closet, and a teenager grabs one and rushes off to school.

In reviewing two books, Rachel Louise Snyder makes the following points: Honest gun owning people play an important role in the murder industry; racism perpetrates a "Southern gun culture"; westerns and other violent media glorify guns; the Second Amendment certifies militias not individual gun owners; "...[C]ourts prohibited private citizens from carrying guns in public, or using them as a weapon against other people"; and she concludes that "The truth is that we live in a world where, despite all we say, our guns say something else."

Reforms and Alternatives

Attempts at gun legislation reform are ongoing but extremely ineffective because pusillanimous federal and state legislators, in thrall to NRA lobbying, fail to do anything as people are constantly murdered. We hear much about mass shootings, especially those that take place at schools, but local individual murders in Alabama or Wyoming do not make the national press. But perhaps not astonishingly, there are often more than (sometimes many more than) 20,000 murders every year in the US. Armaments play a role here. Hold on; there is more: Some 50,000 people commit suicide every year; more than half of these folks use guns. I know this from personal experience and the pain left behind is intolerable and incomprehensible to others. For a detailed overview of our ineffective federal gun control legislation, see <https://en.wikipedia.org/wiki/Gun_law_in_the_United_States#:~:text=Gun%20Control%20Act%20of%201968,Gun%20Control%20Act%20of%201968.>. States, naturally, have their own laws. None of this stops the carnage, especially when the differing voices are so diametrically opposed as in the titles of two articles: "More guns, more crime" vs. "More guns, less crime."

It will take time, but I am convinced that eventually, the law will change matters and private gun ownership will be seriously controlled and immunity for manufacturers and dealers will be repealed. They are, after all, responsible for the harms and deaths that result from the usage of their products.

Minor Reforms

Probably none.

Major Reforms

Jospeh Morelle, Congressman from New York, claims that "I've spent my entire career fighting for gun reform and it's one of my top priorities in Congress." He has co-sponsored at least 14 bills (https://morelle.house.gov/issues/enacting-common-sense-gun-reform). Even when these bills are passed into law, little real prevention occurs which can be seen in the innumerable mass shootings, individual murders, and assassination attempts on various politicians. How can any real progress be made when opponents of gun reform fight back? And mere legislation does no good when individuals subvert the spirit of the law: thus, parents present guns to their teenage children as Christmas presents or miscreants conceal illegal weapons and then use them to cause harm to innocent bystanders.

Radical Reforms

To counter the unequivocal demand of the Second Amendment, there have been some recent laws passed. These include the *Gun Control Act of 1968,* which "regulated interstate and foreign commerce in firearms, including importation, 'prohibited persons', and licensing provisions"; *Brady Handgun Violence* Protection Act of *1993;* and *Bipartisan Safer Communities Act* ("Gun"). See < https://giffords.org/lawcenter/gun-laws/policy-areas/other-laws-policies/key-federal-regulation-acts/> for an annotated list of nine "Key Federal Regulation Acts" and James B. Jacobs and Zoe Fuhr's *The Toughest Gun Control Law in the Nation: The Unfulfilled Promise of New York's SAFE Act,* which indicates that it did not work so well.

International Law

Gun ownership in France (as in all EU countries) is restricted. In order to purchase arms, one must meet certain criteria. In Japan, it is almost impossible for a private individual to purchase or own a gun except for hunting or target practice and these are scrupulously controlled. (In the US in order to purchase a gun, only a cursory online check is necessary to ensure that one is not a felon or lunatic. Additionally, in the US, there are many loopholes.)

Chapter Nine: Incarceration

Definition

Incarceration is the jailing or imprisonment of those who break the law. In order to be incarcerated, one must be accused of a crime (bail/bonded and/or plea-bargained), tried, convicted, and sentenced or fail to make bail. Just how badly this works (and at times not at all) to deny justice can be seen by the plight of the powerful who get away with murder, so to speak.

Those people unfamiliar with police work would be shocked to discover just how many malefactors embezzle, scam, burglarize, rob, mug, abuse, assault, kidnap, rape, and murder. Our fellow human beings really suffer from this onslaught. It is very hard to believe but in 2022, some 16 million crimes were committed in America. And this is why so many people are incarcerated, but also because some cannot post bail; we have almost two million prisoners, which is the most in the world; China is not far behind. Our imprisoned population would be much larger were it not for the bail bonded, plea bargained, probated, and paroled who manage to avoid prison or are released early. There are almost four million probationers and parolees wandering the streets and byways. This is a good thing if all goes well, but horrible if they commit another indiscretion.

Benefits

Incarceration protects the public from additional harm that a criminal might cause. It also acts as a punishment and at times a fear inducing deterrent. It is harmful when the indigent are jailed because they have neither bail money nor collateral.

Detriments

We lock up lots of people. Some are dangerous criminals who, along with Papillon, belong on Devil's Island; others, guilty of little more than a minor traffic violation (or a mere accident), are handcuffed and held in county jails in Virginia, which makes sense, and in Vermont, which does not. About 60 years ago, a friend was assigned to a barracks in Virginia, but liked to return home to New York on weekends. Because the army demands a precise schedule, otherwise one is AWOL, he drove very quickly on this long trip. One day, he found himself flying along at 100 miles an hour, in a little French Simca, when a Virginia officer pulled him over and observed that "You're in a heap of trouble, boy." He had to wait in jail until his wife could wire him the fine money. Much worse is the story of another friend who had an accident and instead of being taken to a hospital was arrested, handcuffed, and driven in a squad car 50 miles from her home and held in jail until I could go north and retrieve her. Vagrants are arrested and homeless are arrested and protesters are arrested, but those who threaten to murder someone are ignored (because they have not acted yet), and violent muggers and murders can post bail!

So, although I am arguing here in favor of incarceration, I also wish to make it clear that far too many American citizens end up in jail or prison. Those guilty of misdemeanors and petty theft should work at normal jobs to repay their victims. If we reserved imprisonment for those who pose a real threat to individuals or society and those who truly deserve punishment (rather than those who cannot post bail), we would have a much smaller prison population. And mandatory sentencing is not necessarily just; leaving decisions to individual (and at times vengeful) judges, is also not beneficial. There is no easy solution to the imprisonment crisis, one that has been going on at least since Jeremy Bentham proposed his Panopticon. (See Foucault's *Discipline and Punish.*)

If incarceration is a major problem in the US, where, you will recall, more people are imprisoned than anywhere else, it also haunts less democratic nations which imprison journalists, writers, dissenters, and everyone else and for long periods under inhumane conditions in concentration camps, Siberia, and notorious penal institutions such as Iran's Evin Prison. As for our enormous prison population, there is a good pragmatic (philosophical) reason for this. Ironically, the US is the world's freest country: We do not require internal passports; we do not have to report to the police upon arriving somewhere, as I did in Innsbruck; unlike in other jurisdictions, under normal circumstances, the military has no warrant in public; and we may do as we wish with little external control. What this means is that we can name our children whatever we desire (try that in France); we can dress as we see fit; in many places we can walk around naked, e.g., a topless woman may legally mosey along New York City's streets. One probably cannot do that in Tehran, eh. So this extreme freedom allows people to act badly and with little fear of horrific consequences, the kind that would occur in Saudi Arabia or even Turkey (see the film *Midnight Express*), not that US prisons are resorts; and so this freedom easily results in bad acts, which in turn lead to incarceration when criminals are caught.

Allied problems include the crowded condition of prisons and inhumane guards who abuse their power, cause real harm and death, and alienate both male and female prisoners. This is why an occasional riot breaks out, like the one in 1971 in Attica, which resulted in the deaths of 43 people including 11 officers. Do not think that this 1971 incident occurred in the distant past and so it has no current standing. In September of 2024, Congolese prisoners in Kinshasa tried to escape because of intolerable conditions in their cells. This resulted in 129 deaths. The good news, despite the rapes, is that more than 700 prisoners were released, most on bail! (Peltier). Like many of the issues discussed in this study, this is an intractable problem—socially and financially. If abundant funds were available, things would be much improved but prison situations will never be perfect because some of the incarcerated are hardened criminals who care little about anyone or anything other than themselves. There will always be trouble in paradise. I wonder how those forgiving philosophers considered above would enjoy living in a community replete with unconfined sex offenders, rapists, murderers, and other dangerous felons. The privatization of prions also harms rather than helps as their owners seek a profit at the expense of the inmates.

Reforms and Alternatives

We often imprison the wrong people for the wrong reasons and in the wrong way. The scammer who bilked a retired lawyer out of some 700,000 dollars should go to prison for a very long time but he should be released daily to earn real money in order to repay his victim. He should spend nights and weekends in Attica, Sing Sing, or Folsom. Far worse is the lunatic who set fire to a California forest in 2024. This arsonist should spend the rest of his life in a federal penitentiary.

And no one should feel sorry for him. Reserve your sympathy for the thousands of acres, houses, and animals he destroyed. Bear in mind that 15 percent of California wildfires are set by arsonists Many others are caused by careless humans.

The famous and wealthy often manage to avoid imprisonment. In 2024 Justin Timberlake was arrested for driving while under the influence of alcohol. Naturally, he bargained his way to a lesser admission and was fined $500, required to do community service, and had a brief license revocation. Timberlake is worth 250 million dollars. Does a $500 fine make sense? What if he had killed someone? Would a guilty migrant in Sag Harbor, an area in the infamously wealthy Long Island Hamptons, be in jail? Well, of course.

The US spends almost 200 billion dollars a year to incarcerate two million people, far too many criminals (and others), so reforming the system is a truly pressing necessity and many agree, so that unlike some of the other procedures criticized in this monograph, beneficial reforms to incarceration are ongoing, and the enormous periodical and monographic literature reflects this.

Minor Reforms

"The need for comprehensive sentencing reform is clear, but political limits on legislative remedies and the failure of the courts to notably reduce the scale, or improve conditions, of confinement render these approaches highly uncertain. In the short term, unconventional methods that do not require legislative authorization, such as electing, pressuring, and incentivizing prosecutors to reduce penal severity, may be a promising way of addressing mass incarceration. The return and revitalization of parole or other systems of post-sentence review are also crucial and may be legitimated in terms of the need to incentivize rehabilitation and prevent the unnecessary and costly incarceration of the elderly. The recent mobilization of grass-roots movements for penal change that include those directly affected by both violence and mass incarceration is also auspicious, as their work may help to humanize the justice-involved and undermine the erroneous assumption that crime survivors are well-served by mass incarceration" (Beckett, abstract 235). If these and other suggestions were implemented, things would improve.

And again, "State lawmakers in New Mexico adopted Senate Bill

29 which made several changes to the state's medical and geriatric parole system…; similar reforms were advanced in North Carolina; "California, Colorado, and Minnesota adopted or expanded second look policies"; voting, clean slate, and youth parole eligibility and sentencing reform were also altered; note that "Youth incarceration declined 75% between 2000 and 2022" (Porter). These actions are all praiseworthy but they are minor alterations to an enormous systemic problem that requires major attitudinal and policy changes. The many small alterations help, but they are not enough. Somehow, societal changes in attitude toward the poor, minorities, immigrants, and others must take place, if we are to decrease our enormous incarcerated population. At least the FCC finally mandated that prison phone calls be priced at a reasonable rather than an exorbitant rate.

Here is another take: "This manuscript uses data drawn from case studies of New Jersey, Pennsylvania, Illinois, and Michigan from 2000 to 2006 in order to examine how different states responded to mounting problems caused by mass incarceration. Lawmakers and penal administrators inherited correctional systems that had at least doubled in size over the previous decade and faced budgetary problems, overcrowded conditions, and federal litigation. When economic pressures and the 2001 recession destabilized state budgets, state officials responded differently to these crises. While legislators remained committed to the carceral ethos that had driven prison expansion, some governors and penal administrators charged with managing state corrections systems began to consider new responses that moved away from prison expansion. As we show, executives and penal administrators in some states successfully implemented reforms by making changes to back-end correctional processes. Their successes highlight the importance of autonomy from external pressures that allowed some administrators to respond to mounting problems in ways that reduced their state's reliance on imprisonment. These administrators deployed their correctional expertise to pursue policies that minimized political backlash. States lacking the necessary institutional structures and sufficient external pressures largely sustained the penal status quo" (Schoenfeld, abstract 482).

Major Reforms

Sarah Staudt discusses 32 potential reforms for reducing

incarceration under nine headings including the following: "Reduce the number of people entering the 'revolving doors' of jails and prisons," "Reduce the footprint of probation and parole systems..." "Protect incarcerated people and families from exploitation," and "Eliminate relics of the harmful and racist 'war on drugs.'" The precise and detailed changes noted are extremely beneficial but if they are only suggestions rather than implemented legislation, they are not truly useful. And of course only specific states pass such laws, which means that the (potentially) incarcerated in other states fare no better than they did in the past.

Radical Reforms

By "strengthening the Federal Bureau of Prisons," officials hope to reduce recidivism. They will identify the inmate's criminogenic needs; create a school district in the system; educate inmates; create job skills; emphasize mental health and family ties; reduce solitary confinement; eliminate private prisons; and implement other improvements. ("Prison"). These are all extremely beneficial and will have a positive effect. The Brennan Center for Justice has suggested a radical change: "For decades, the federal government used its grant-making power to spur states to incarcerate more people and to impose longer sentences. It should now use that power to reverse course." This proposal contains a model Bill (Stroud). Indeed!

International law

It is obvious that incarceration is extremely complex globally. In France, at least criminals are no longer sent to Devil's Island, but prisons are overcrowded and conditions are not good. Japan imprisons those who deserve it; labor is required; and the system is rather repressive.

Conclusion

The law should benefit the people; benefits to the state should be of secondary importance. But as it happens, over the centuries, legal strictures that are useful to the state *or to no one* have been emplaced by overzealous, religious, bigoted, or corrupt legislators or misguided justices (at all levels), who have created harmful precedents that nevertheless control future judicial decisions. Truly bizarre laws include the following: In Delaware, it is illegal to sell pet fur and this indiscretion carries a $2500 fine as well as an inability to own a dog or cat; in Idaho, "cannibalism is *usually* illegal"; in Louisiana, "jambalaya is not subject to state sanitary code"; in Nevada, pedoscopes (to measure feet) are illegal; in North Carolina, it is illegal to plow cotton fields using elephants; in North Dakota, it is illegal to fall asleep with one's shoes on; and in Utah, it is illegal to bite someone while boxing (https://thelawdictionary.org/article/weird-laws-by-state/). How can justice prevail when legislators pass such preposterous (and ultimately harmful) laws? Federal legislation should, generally, replace divergent and overabundant state statutes.

I have discussed legal problems above in the hope that a more enlightened Congress and Supreme Court will alter matters so that justice may prevail, although it will be many years before things improve. At a time when a substantial minority of citizens (about one third of the eligible population) do not bother to vote, or vote for bizarre candidates (such as Ralph Nader or Robert F. Kennedy, Jr.) who draw votes away from a legitimate candidate, or choose to elect an oligarch who causes extreme global harm, it is no wonder that things will be appalling for the people and the environment well into the foreseeable future.

Appendix A: Federal and State Legislation

Presenting some federal laws for this study's issues may prove helpful in understanding what I have offered above. But it makes little sense to include too many of the differing laws that one will find in the 50 states' statutes and so only a handful of these are enumerated in order to exemplify the diverse nature of state law. All laws cited in the text plus many others are included here.

Federal Legislation

Bail/Bonding

Bail does not exist for federal crimes in the same way that it does for those committed at the state level.

The Bail Reform Act of 1966. 80 STAT. PUBLIC LAW 89-465-JUNE 22, 1966

The Bail Reform Act of 1984. 18 U.S.C. § 3142 (repeals the 1966 act)

Bail Bond Fairness Act.

Plea Bargaining

The 14th Amendment to the Constitution: Amdt14.S1.5.5.4 Plea Bargaining in Pre-Trial Process

Speedy Trial Act of 1974 88 Stat. 2080, as amended August 2, 1979, 93 Stat. 328, 18 U.S.C. §§ 3161–3174

First Step Act (2018) Public Law 115–391

Probation/Parole

Probationers and Parolees 18 U.S. Code § 3522

Sentencing Reform Act of 1984 98-473, title II, ch. II (Sec. 211 et seq.)

Incest

There is no federal legislation against incest.

Prostitution

There is no federal legislation banning prostitution per se.

Assisted suicide

Assisted suicide Public law 105–12—Apr. 30, 1997 111 Stat. 23

Abortion

Women's Health Protection Act of 2021.

Ensuring Access to Abortion Act of 2022.

Guns

Gun Control Act of 1968 PUBLIC LAW 90-618-OCT. 22, 1968 82 Stat

Firearms Owners; Protection Act of 1986 PUBLIC LAW 99-308—MAY 19, 1986 100 STAT. 449

Brady Handgun Violence Prevention Act of 1993. 103-159, title I, 1993-11-30, 107 Stat. 1536 (18 U.S.C. 921 note)

Bipartisan Safer Communities Act PUBLIC LAW 117–159—JUNE 25, 2022. 136 STAT. 1313

State Legislation

Bail/Bonding

SAFE-T Act. [Illinois].

Pretrial Fairness Act. {Illinois}.

A. VERMONT STATUTES ANNOTATED TITLE THIRTEEN. Crimes and Criminal Procedure PART 5. JUDGMENT AND PROCEEDINGS AFTER JUDGMENT CHAPTER 229. Bail and Recognizances

Idaho Bail Act Idaho Code Title 19, Chapter 29 (2023)

Plea Bargaining

Arkansas Victim Rights LawAct 1262 of 1997

Appeal of Sentence Alaska Stat. § 1255.120

Probation

Conditions of probation ORS 137.540 [Oregon]

Supervision on probation, MCA46-23-1011 [Montana]

Parole

General Conditions of parole 37 Pa. Code § 63.4 [Pennsylvania]

2023 Delaware Code
Title 11. Crimes and Criminal Procedure
Chapter 43. Sentencing probation, parole, and pardons
Subchapter II. Probation and Parole Services
§ 4321. Probation and parole officers.

The Less Is More: Community Supervision Revocation Reform

Act (S1144A/A5576A) [New York]

Prostitution

Prostitution—after positive HIV test Section 2907.25 [Ohio]

Incest

Incest 76-7-102 (Utah)

Incest 97-29-27 (Mississippi)

Assisted suicide

Assisting suicide Iowa Code Section 707A.2

Abortion

Title 22: HEALTH AND WELFARE Subtitle 2: HEALTH Part 3: PUBLIC HEALTH Chapter 263-B: ABORTIONS §1599 [Maine]

Gun legislation

Sullivan Act 134th sess.: I. 1911. pp. 442–445. [New York]

Appendix B: Federal and State Court Cases

All cases cited in the text plus many others are included here.

Federal Court Cases

Bail/Bonding

United States v. Salerno 481 U.S. 739 (1987)

Plea Bargaining

Bordenkircher v, Hayes 434 US 357 (1978)

North Carolina v. Alford 91 S.Ct. 160 (1970)

Shelton v. United States 242 F.2d 101, 113 (5th Cir. 1957).

(See < https://barkanresearch.com/top-plea-bargaining-cases/> for an annotated list of 10 influential federal plea bargaining cases.)

Probation

UNITED STATES V. KNIGHTS (00-1260) 534 U.S. 112 (2001)

Gagnon v. Scarpelli 411 U.S. 778 (1973)

Parole

Morrissey v. Brewer, 408 U.S. 471 (1972)

Prostitution

United States v. Bitty208 U.S. 393 (1908)

California v. Freeman488 U.S. 1311 (1989)

Incest

Lawrence v. Texas539 U.S. 558 (2003)

United States of America v. Walter E. Ashe 427 F.2d 626 (D.C. Cir. 1970)

Assisted suicide

Washington v. Glucksberg
521 U.S. 702 (1997)

Vacco v. Quill
521 U.S. 793 (1997)

Abortion

Roe v. Wade 410 U.S. 113 (1973) assisted suicode

Statutory Rape

Orr v. Orr440 U.S. 268 (1979)

Incarceration

Miller v. Alabama567 U.S. 460 (2012)

Bassett v. Arizona.603 U. S. ____ (2024)

Other

Korematsu v. US 323 U.S. 214 (1944)

Buck v. Bell274 U.S. 200 (1927)

Marbury v. Madison5 U.S. 137 (1803)

Loving v. Virginia388 U.S. 1 (1967)

State Court Cases

Listed below are a small sampling of state cases.

Bail/Bonding

Vermont: State v. Jones 167 Vt. 615, 709 A.2d 507

State v. Fernald 168 Vt. 620, 723 A 2d 1134

Bondsman, Inc. v. Taylor367 Ga.App. 213,885 S.E.2d 249

Action Bail Bonds v. State WY 103 49 P.3d 992

Johnson Bonding Co., Inc. v. Com. of KY 420 F. Supp. 331 (E.D. Ky. 1976)

Plea Bargaining

Davis v. State625 N.W. 2d 855 [North Dakota]

State v. Comer 584 A.2d 638 (1990) [Maine]

The State of South Carolina, Secondary Appellant, v. BECKA (1999) State, 297 S.C. 52, 374 S.E.2d 683 (1988)

Probation

State ex rel. Holman v. Ohio Adult Parole Auth. 171 Ohio St.3d 806, 2023-Ohio-692

Anaya v. State96 Nev. 119

Parole

State ex rel. Brust v. Chambers-Smith 156 Ohio St. 3d 331, 2019-Ohio-857

Villery v. Florida Parole & Probation Com'n396 So. 2d 1107

(1980)

Prostitution

Court upholds NY prostitution laws—Cherry v. Koch126 A.D.2d 346, 514 N.Y.S.2d 30 (N.Y.A.D. 2 Dept. 1987)

Incest

State v. Johnson 269 Neb. 507 (2005)

Assisted suicide

State v. Melchert-Dinkel. 844 NW 2d 13 - Minn: Supreme Court, 2014

Abortion

Helen Weems v. State of Montana50-20-109(1)(a)

Other

Illinois v. Nathan Leopold and Richard Loeb No court case citation is available

References

Be aware that there exist many thousands of apposite web sites as well as scholarly papers and books (both accessible on Google Scholar and Google Books) plus discussions on Google's Forums as well as books collected in libraries and hundreds of videos on *YouTube* on all of the legal boondoggles discussed in this study. The extensive reference list appended below represents a small percentage of available material.

Abagnale, Frank W. *Catch Me If You Can.* New York: Broadway Books, 2002.

Alkon, Cynthia. "What's Law Got to Do with It? Plea Bargaining Reform after Lafler and Frye." *Arbitration Law Review* 7: *Yearbook on Arbitration and Mediation* 1 (2015). https://elibrary.law.psu.edu/cgi/viewcontent.cgi?article=1027&context=arbitrationlawreview

Annison, Jill, Tina Eadie, and Charlotte Knight. "People First: Probation Officer Perspectives on Probation Work" *Probation Journal* 55.3 (September 1, 2008).

"Bail in the United States." *Wikipedia* 22 May 2024. https://en.wikipedia.org/wiki/Bail_in_the_United_States:

The Bail Project 2024. https://bailproject.org/

Baker, Shannon M., Michael S. Vaughn, and Volkan Topalli. "A review of the powers of bail bond agents and bounty hunters: Exploring legalities and illegalities of quasi-criminal justice officials." *Aggression and Violent Behavior* 13.2, March-April 2008: 124-130. https://www.sciencedirect.com/science/article/abs/pii/S1359178908000050

Bagaric, Mirko, Julie Clarke, and William Rininger. "Plea Bargaining: From Patent Unfairness to Transparent Justice." *Missouri Law Review* 84.1 (Winter 2019): 1-46. https://scholarship.law.missouri.edu/cgi/viewcontent.cgi?article=4364&context=mlr

Bailey, V. and S. McCabe. "Reforming the Law of Incest. *Criminal Law Review.* December 1979: 749-764. https://www.ojp.gov/

ncjrs/virtual-library/abstracts/reforming-law-incest

Baughman, Shima Baradaran. *The Bail Book: A Comprehensive Look at Bail in America's Criminal Justice System.* New York: Cambridge UP, 2018. https://www.google.com/books/edition/The_Bail_Book/La8_DwAAQBAJ?hl=en&gbpv=1

Beckett, Katherine. "The Politics, Promise, and Peril of Criminal Justice Reform in the Context of Mass Incarceration." *Annual Review of Criminology* 1 (2018): 235-259. https://lsj.washington.edu/sites/lsj/files/documents/research/annual_review_of_criminology_2018.pdf

Bibas, Stephanos. "Incompetent Plea Bargaining and Extrajudicial Reforms." *Harvard Law Review* 126 (2012): 150 -174. https://scholarship.law.upenn.edu/cgi/viewcontent.cgi?article=1459&&context=faculty_scholarship&&sei-redir=1&referer=https%253A%252F%252Fscholar.google.com%252Fscholar%253Fhl%253Den%2526as_sdt%253D0%25252C46%2526q%253Dplea%252Bbargaining%252Breform%2526btnG%253D#search=%22plea%20bargaining%20reform%22

Billings, Thanithia. "Private Interest, Public Sphere: Eliminating the Use of Commercial Bail Bondsmen in the Criminal Justice System." *Boston College Law Review* 57.4 (September 2016): 1336-1365. https://core.ac.uk/download/pdf/71468382.pdf

Blow, Charles M. "Two Governors, Two Visions of a New South." *The New York Times*, 26 June 2024. https://www.nytimes.com/2024/06/26/opinion/wes-moore-jeff-landry-maryland-louisiana.html?searchResultPosition=1

Bond, James E. *Plea Bargaining and Guilty Pleas.* New York: Clark Boardman Co., 1975.

Brand, Jessica and Jessica Pishko. "Bail Reform: Explained." *The Appeal*, 14 June 2018. https://theappeal.org/bail-reform-explained-4abb73dd2e8a/

Brickner, Mike. "Probation Reform: What's Ahead and How You Can Help." ACLU Delaware, 2 July 2024. https://www.aclu-de.org/en/news/probation-reform-whats-ahead-and-how-you-can-help

Brock, David *Stench: The Making of the Thomas Court and the Unmaking of America.* New York: Alfred A. Knopf, 2024.

Brown, Elizabeth Nolan. "States Try To Reform Prostitution Laws—for Better and Worse." *Reason Magazine, 17* March 2023. https://reason.com/2023/03/17/states-try-to-reform-prostitution-laws-for-better-and-worse/

Canton, Rob and Jane Dominey. *Probation.* 2nd ed. London: Routledge. 2017. https://www.taylorfrancis.com/books/mono/10.4324/9781315407029/probation-rob-canton-jane-dominey

Chokshi, Niraj. "U.S. Said to Seek Boeing Guilty Plea to Avoid Trial in 737 Max Crashes." *The New York Times,* 30 June 2024. https://www.nytimes.com/2024/06/30/business/boeing-max-justice-department.html?searchResultPosition=1

Cocca, Carolyn E. "Prosecuting Mrs. Robinson? Gender, Sexuality, and Statutory Rape Laws." *Michigan Feminist Studies,* 16 (2002). https://quod.lib.umich.edu/cgi/t/text/text-idx?cc=mfsfront;c=mfs;c=mfsfront;idno=ark5583.0016.003;g=mfsg;rgn=main;view=text;xc=1

Colb, Sherry F. "The pros and cons of statutory rape laws." *CNN.com,* 13 February 2004. https://www.cnn.com/2004/LAW/02/13/findlaw.analysis.colb.statutory.rape/index.html

Crowley, Kinsey. "Two years ago, SCOTUS overturned the right to an abortion. Here is how each state changed." *USA Today,* 24 June 2024. https://www.usatoday.com/story/news/politics/2024/06/23/state-by-state-abortion-laws-dobbs-anniversary/73769814007/

Davis, Robert S. and Lee I. Correa. *Bil Bond Handbook.* Austin: Texas Association of Counties, 2023. https://countyorgprodblob2023.blob.core.usgovcloudapi.net/cms/tac/media/default/member-services/legal/legal-publications/bail-bond-handbook.pdf

Dervan, Lucian E. "Fourteen Principles and a Path Forward for Plea Bargaining Reform." *Criminal Justice 3*8.4, January 22, 2024. (https://www.americanbar.org/groups/criminal_justice/publications/ criminal-justice-magazine/2024/winter/fourteen-principles-path-forward-plea-bargaining-reform/).

Devine, Francis Edward. "Outlawing Commercial Bail Bonding: A Comparative Perspective." *The Anglo American Law Review,* 31 December 1987. https://typeset.io/papers/outlawing-commercial-bail-bonding-a-comparative-perspective-1h6i544jyq

Dias, Elizabeth and Lisa Lerer. *The Fall of Roe: The Rise of a New America.* New York: Flatiron Books, 2024.

Dressler, David. *Practice and Theory of Probation and Parole.* 2nd ed. New York: Columbia UP, 1969 (1951).

"Drug Law Reform," National Association of Criminal Defense Lawyers. https://www.nacdl.org/Landing/DrugLaw#:~:text=NACDL%20calls%20upon%20the%20federal,and%20delivery%20of%20controlled%20substances.
"Drug Policy Reform," Amnesty International. https://www.amnesty.org/en/what-we-do/drug-policy-reform/
Dworkin, Ronald, Thomas Nigel, Robert Nozick, John Rawls, et al. "Assisted Suicide: The Philosophers' Brief." *The New York Review of Books,* 27 March 1997: 1-17. https://core.ac.uk/reader/31066630
Eidson, R. "Constitutionality of Statutory Rape Laws." *UCLA Law Review* 27.3 (February 1980): 757-815. https://www.ojp.gov/ncjrs/virtual-library/abstracts/constitutionality-statutory-rape-laws
Esthappan, Sino and Janine Zweig. "Advancing Probation Reform: A Deep-End Evaluation Feature Brief." Urban Institute. September 2020. (1-11). https://www.urban.org/sites/default/files/publication/102768/advancing-probation-reform.pdf
Fadel, Alexis and Avery Fadel. "Plea Bargaining Reforms to Protect Innocent People." The Center for Growth and Opportunity, 13 June 2023. https://www.thecgo.org/benchmark/plea-bargaining-reforms-to-protect-innocent-people/#:~:text=Limiting%20the%20number%20of%20plea%20deals%20that%20can%20be%20offered,credible%20evidence%20for%20a%20conviction
Fisher, George. *Plea Bargaining's Triumph: A History of Plea Bargaining in America.* Stanford: University Press, 2003.
Foucault, Michel. *Discipline and Punish: The Birth of the Prison* New York: Vintage Books, 1995 (1976).
Freed, Daniel and Patricia M. Wald. B*ail in the United States, 1964.* Washington, DC: United Sates Department of Justice and the Vera Foundation, 1964.
Gabriel, Trip. "James C. Scott, Iconoclastic Social Scientist, Dies at 87. *The New York Times* 28 (29) July, 2024. https://www.nytimes.com/2024/07/28/books/james-scott-dead.html
Gabrieli, Lilla, and 14 additional authors. "Reforming Parole for Life Sentence with Parole: A Commission Presented to the Sentencing Project." Harvard IOP [Institute of Politics] June 2019: 1-65. https://iop.harvard.edu/sites/default/files/2023-02/IOP_Policy_Program_2019_Life_Sentences_w_Parole.pdf
Golden, Marilyn and Tyler Zoanni. "Killing Us Softly: The dangers of

legalizing assisted suicide." *Disability and Health Journal* 3 (2010): 16-30. https://citeseerx.ist.psu.edu/document?repid=rep1&type=pdf&doi=8a0f0d862a9348c8d66d98c60d86feece3d28120

Goodwin, Michelle. "Law's Limits: Regulating Statutory Rape Law." *Wisconsin Law Review,* 2013: 481-540. https://wlr.law.wisc.edu/wp-content/uploads/sites/1263/2013/05/6-Goodwin-2.pdf

Green, Stuart P. "How to Criminalize Incest." SSRN 11 (15) May 2017. https://ssrn.com/abstract=2967280

"Gun Control Act." ATF 21 October 2022. https://www.atf.gov/rules-and-regulations/gun-control-act

Harrison, Kathryn. *The Kiss: A Memoir.* New York: Random House, 1997.

Haugeberg, Karissa. *Woman Against Abortion: Inside the Largest Moral Reform Movement of the Twentieth Century. Champaign:* University of Illinois, 2017.

Hauptman, Robert. *Debunking Scholarly Nonsense.* Washington, DC: Academica, 2022.

Hennes, Erin P. And Layla Dang. "The Devil We Know: Legal Precedent and the Preservation of Injustice." *Policy Insights from the Behavioral and Brain Sciences* 8.1 (February 11, 2021). https://journals.sagepub.com/doi/10.1177/2372732220980757

Hernández, Amanda. "Cash bail policies are under fresh scrutiny." *Stateline* 30.2, 13 November 2023. https://stateline.org/2023/11/13/cash-bail-policies-are-under-fresh-scrutiny/

Herzog-Evans, Martine. "Probation in France: Some things old, some things new, some things borrowed, and often blue." *Probation Journal* 58.4 (2011): 345-354. https://globcci.org/wp-content/uploads/2021/08/Probation-in-France-2011.pdf

Heumann, Milton. *Plea Bargaining: The Experiences of Prosecutors, Judges, and Defense Attorneys.* Chicago: University of Chicago, 1978.

Highmore, A., Jr. A *Digest of the Doctrine of Bail in Civil and Criminal Cases.* London: T. Cadell, 1783. https://www.google.com/books/edition/A_Digest_of_the_Doctrine_of_Bail_in_Civi/jLADAAAAQAAJ?hl=en&gbpv=1&dq=bail+bonding&printsec=frontcover

Jacobs, James B. and Zoe Fuhr. *The Toughest Gun Control Law in the Nation: The Unfulfilled Promise of New York's SAFE Act.* New York: New York University Press, 2019.

Jorgensen, Isabella and Sandra Susan Smith. "The Current State of Bail Reform in the United States: Results of a Landscape Analysis of Bail Reforms Across All 50 States." HKS Faculty Research Working Paper Series RWP21-033, December 2021. https://dash.harvard.edu/bitstream/handle/1/37370366/RWP21-033_Smith.pdf?sequence=3

"Justice Without Retribution." *Neuroethics* 13.1, April 2020. *https://link.springer.com/journal/12152/volumes-and-issues/13-1*

Kato, Saki. "Probation in Japan: Engaging the Community." *Irish Probation Journal* 15 (October 2018): 114-136. https://www.probation.ie/EN/PB/0/4B3BF8484A4F1E638025834E004BFD70/$File/Kato_Saki_IPJ.pdf

Kelly, Patrick and Don Stemen. "Probation Reform: Is Zero Tolerance a Viable Option?" Vera Institute of Justice: "Research and Practice Forum." October 2005. (1-8). https://www.vera.org/downloads/publications/Probation_reform.pdf

Kelly, William R. with Robert Pitman. *Confronting Underground Justice: Reinventing Plea Bargaining for Effective Criminal Justice Reform.* Lanham, MD: Rowman & Littlefield, 2018.

Kershnar, Stephen. "Should Statutory Rape Be a Crime?" *The Palgrave Handbook of Sexual Ethics.* New York: Palgrave Macmillan, 2022. 8 February 2022. (339-356). *https://link.springer.com/chapter/10.1007/978-3-030-87786-6_20*

Kluft, Richard P. "Ramifications of Incest." *Psychiatric Times* 27.12 (January 12, 2011). *https://www.psychiatrictimes.com/view/ramifications-incest*

Laband. David N. et al. *Blue Laws: The History, Economics, and Politics of Sunday-Closing Laws.* Lexington, MA: Lexington Books, 1987.

Lawson, Gary S. "The Constitutional Case against Precedent." *Harvard Journal of Law & Public Policy* 23 (Winter 1994). *https://scholarship.law.bu.edu/cgi/viewcontent.cgi?article=3554&context=faculty_scholarship*

Lewis, Jonathan, et al. "Pathways to Drug Liberalization: Racial Justice, Public Health, and Human Rights." *The American Journal of Bioethics* 22.9 (June 30 2021): W10-W12. *https://philarchive.org/archive/LEWPTD-2*

Liebermann, Oren and Lauren del Valle. "US reaches plea deal with alleged 9/11 mastermind Khalid Sheikh Mohammed." *CNN* 1,

August 2024. https://www.cnn.com/2024/07/31/politics/us-plea-deal-9-11-mastermind-khalid-sheikh-mohammed/index.html

Lippke, Richard L. *The Ethics of Plea Bargaining.* New York: Oxford UP, 2011.

Liptak, Adam. "Long Prison Terms Deserve a Second Look and 'a Little Humanity,' Judge Argues." *The New York Times* 9 September 2024. https://www.nytimes.com/2024/09/09/us/federal-sentencing-first-step-act.html?searchResultPosition=1

Londoño, Ernesto. "Nixon Started the War on Drugs. Privately, He Said Pot Was 'Not Particularly Dangerous.'" *The New York Times,* 14 September 2024. https://www.nytimes.com/2024/09/14/us/nixon-marijuana-tapes.html

Lovins, Brian K., Lori A. Brusman Lovins, and Edward J. Latessa. "Reimagining Probation Reform: Applying a Coaching Model to Probation Departments." In Jeglic, E., Calkins, C., eds. *Handbook of Issues in Criminal Justice Reform in the United States.* Cham, Switzerland: Springer, Cham, 2022. December 5, 2021. (291–305). https://link.springer.com/chapter/10.1007/978-3-030-77565-0_16

Lubin, Gus. "10 Super Rich Guys Who Jumped Bail." *Business Insider,* 11 May 2011. https://www.businessinsider.com/guys-who-jumped-bail-2011-5

Mandel, Michael. "Rethinking Parole." *Osgoode Hall Law Journal* 13.2 (1975): 501-546. https://digitalcommons.osgoode.yorku.ca/cgi/viewcontent.cgi?article=2214&&context=ohlj&&sei-redir=1&referer=https%253A%252F%252Fscholar.google.com%252Fscholar%253Fhl%253Den%2526as_sdt%253D0%25252C46%2526q%253Dparole%252B%2526btnG%253D#search=%22parole%22

Mantle, Desmond. "Fixing the Plea Bargaining Process Is an Essential Criminal Justice Reform." Reason Foundation 3 March 2022. https://reason.org/commentary/fixing-the-plea-bargaining-process-is-an-essential-criminal-justice-reform/

Marchese, Nino, Matthew Grady, and Michael Bosset. "Embracing Parole Reform Across the States." American Legislative Exchange Council, 5 October 2021. https://alec.org/article/embracing-parole-reform-across-the-states/

Monasky, Heather. "Note: On Comprehensive Prostitution Reform: Criminalizing the Trafficker and the Trick, but Not the Victim—

Sweden's Sexköpslagen in America," *William Mitchell Law Review* 37. 4 (2011): 1-57. http://open.mitchellhamline.edu/wmlr/vol37/iss4/8

"Navigating State-Specific Bail Laws and Their Variations." *AAAA Discount Bail Bonds,* 2024. https://aaaabailbonds.com/2024/04/18/navigating-state-specific-bail-laws-and-theirvariations#:~:text=The%20key%20differences%20in%20bail%20regulations%20across%20states%20extend%20beyond,defendants%20in%20the%20bail%20process

"New Neport: A blueprint for meaningful probation and parole reform in Connecticut—and other states." Prison Policy Initiative, 23 May 2023. https://www.prisonpolicy.org/blog/2023/05/23/probation-parole-reforms/

"New York's New Bail Reform Model: The next wave of bail reform goes beyond ending money bail." State of Justice Reform, 2019. Vera Institute. https://www.vera.org/state-of-justice-reform/2019/bail-reform

Olszewski, Daryl J. "Statutory Rape in Wisconsin: History, Rationale, and the Need for Reform." *Marquette Law Review* 89.3 (Spring 2006): 693-719. https://scholarship.law.marquette.edu/cgi/viewcontent.cgi?referer=&httpsredir=1&article=1114&context=mulr

"Oregon Rethinks Drug Decriminalization." (Editorial opinion.) *The Wall Street Journal,* 30 January 2024: A14.

Peltier, Elian. "Congo Releases More Than 700 Inmates After a Deadly Stampede." *The New York Times,* 22 September 2024. https://www.nytimes.com/2024/09/22/world/africa/congo-prison-release.html

Petersilla, Joan. "When Probation Becomes More Dreaded Than Prison." *Federal Probation Journal* 54 (1990): 23-27. https://heinonline.org/HOL/LandingPage?handle=hein.journals/fedpro54&div=7&id=&page=

Petersilla, Joan, Susan Turner, James Kahan, and Joyce Peterson. *Granting Felons Probation: Public Risks and Alternatives.* Np: National Institute of Justice: US Department of Justice, 1985.

Phelps, Michelle S. "Ending Mass Probation: Sentencing, Supervision, and Revocation." *The Future of Children* 28.1 (Spring 2018): 125-146. https://files.eric.ed.gov/fulltext/EJ1179164.pdf

Plotkin, S. J. *Get Bail, Leave Jail: America's Guide to Hiring a Bondsman, Navigating Bail Bonds, and Getting Out of Custody Before Trial.* Buffalo: Identity Publications, 2021. *https://www.google.com/books/edition/Get_Bail_Leave_Jail/KKi1zgEACAAJ?hl=en*

Porter, Nicole D. "Top Trends in Criminal Legal Reform, 2023." The Sentencing Project, 20 December 2023. https://www.sentencingproject.org/publications/top-trends-in-criminal-legal-reform-2023/

Preston, Allie. *Fact Sheet: The Case for Cash Bail Reform.* Center for American Progress, 9 August 2023. https://www.americanprogress.org/article/the-case-for-cash-bail-reform/

Preston, Allie, and Rachael Eisenberg. *Fact Sheet: Profit Over People: Inside the Commercial Bail Bond Industry Fueling America's Cash Bail Systems.* Center for American Progress, 6 July 2022. https://www.americanprogress.org/article/fact-sheet-profit-over-people/

"Prison Reform: Reducing Recidivism by Strengthening the Federal Bureau of Prisons." U.S. Department of Justice, 29 November 2023. https://www.justice.gov/archives/prison-reform

"Probation and Parole." National Institute of Corrections. https://nicic.gov/resources/resources-topics-and-roles/topics/probation-and-parole#:~:text=Probation%20is%20a%20sentence%20handed,in%20a%20jail%20or%20prison.

Rakove, Jack. "The Justices Are Bad Gun Historians." *The Wall Street Journal,* 2 November 2023. https://www.wsj.com/us-news/law/the-justices-are-bad-gun-historians-8fcc05c7?st=my59gqryprtt9mf&reflink=desktopwebshare_permalink

Rawls, John. *A Theory of Justice.* Cambridge: Harvard UP, 1971.

Raymond, Janice G. "Ten Reasons for Not Legalizing Prostitution and a Legal Response to the Demand for Prostitution." *Journal of Trauma Practice* 2, 2003: 315-332. https://www.antiprostitutie.ro/docs/10.Reasons.for.Not.Legalizing.Prostitution.pdf

Reuter, Peter. "Why Has US Drug Policy Changed So Little over 30 Years?" *Crime and Justice 42* (May 21, 2013): 1-67. (75-140). https://reuter.it-prod-webhosting.aws.umd.edu/sites/default/files/reuter/files/proofs_corrected.pdf

Richer, Alanna Durkin et al. "What to Know About the Supreme Court Immunity Ruling in Trump's 2020 Election Interference Case." *AP* 1 July 2024. https://apnews.com/article/trump-immunity-supreme-court-capitol-riot-trial-72ec35de776315183e

1db561257cb108

Richtel, Matt. "Does Legalizing Cannabis Increase Adolescent Use? This Expert Found Mixed Results." *The New York Times* 20 May 2024. https://www.nytimes.com/2024/05/20/health/marijuana-weed-adolescents-coley.html?searchResultPosition=1

Rolles, Steve. *Legalizing Drugs: The Key to Ending the War.* Oxford: New International Publications, 2017.

Rosen, Jeffrey. "Prisoners of Parole." *The New York Times Magazine,* 8 January 2010. https://www.nytimes.com/2010/01/10/magazine/10prisons-t.html

Rosenbaum, Thane. *The Myth of Moral Justice: Why Our Legal System Fails to Do What's Right.* New York: HarperCollins, 2004.

Rosenbaum, Thane. *Payback: The Case for Revenge.* Chicago: University of Chicago, 2013.

Rosenberg, Carol. "Defense Secretary Revokes Plea Deal for Accused Sept. 11 Plotters" *The New York Times,* 2 August 2024. https://www.nytimes.com/2024/08/02/us/politics/911-plotters-plea-deal.html

Rosett, Arthur and Donald R. Cressey. *Justice by Consent: plea bargains in the American courthouse.* New York: J.B. Lippincott, 1976.

Schaeffer, Katherine. "Key facts about Americans and guns." Pew Research Center, 24 July 2024. https://www.pewresearch.org/short-reads/2024/07/24/key-facts-about-americans-and-guns/

Schoenfeld, Heather and Michael C. Campbell. "Early 21st Century Penal Reform: A Comparative Analysis of Four States' Responses to the Problems of Mass Incarceration." *Law & Policy* 45.4 (2023): 482–506. https://www.researchgate.net/profile/Heather-Schoenfeld/publication/371687642_Early_21st_century_penal_reform_A_comparative_analysis_of_four_states%27_responses_to_the_problems_of_mass_incarceration/links/667efb762aa57f3b825dc55c/Early-21st-century-penal-reform-A-comparative-analysis-of-four-states-responses-to-the-problems-of-mass-incarceration.pdf

Scott-Hayward, Christine S. "The Failure of Parole: Rethinking the Role of the State in Reentry." *New Mexico Law Review* 41.2 (Fall 2011): 421-465. https://digitalrepository.unm.edu/cgi/viewcontent.cgi?article=1098&&context=nmlr&&sei-redir=1&referer=https%253A%252F%252Fscholar.google.com%252Fschol

ar%253Fstart%253D70%2526q%253Dparole%2526hl%253Den%2526as_sdt%253D0%252C46#search=%22parole%22

Siegel, Joshua S. et al. "Psychedelics Drug Legislative Reform and Legalization in the US." *JAMA Psychiatry* 80.1 (January 1, 2023): 77-83. https://www.ncbi.nlm.nih.gov/pmc/articles/PMC10069558/

Smith, Steve. "Leslie Van Houten Parole Was a Tragic Mistake." *PRI,* 31 July 2023. https://www.pacificresearch.org/leslie-van-houten-parole-was-a-tragic-mistake/

Snyder, Rachel Louise. "An America Where Guns Do the Talking." Review of *One Nation Under Guns: How Gun Culture Distorts Our History and Threatens Our Democracy* by Dominic Erdozain and *What We've Become: Living and Dying in a Country of Arms* by Jonathan M. Metzl. *The New York Times,* 8 February 2024. https://www.nytimes.com/2024/01/30/books/review/one-nation-under-guns-dominic-erdozain-what-weve-become-jonathan-metzl.html

"States Can Shorten Probation and Protect Public Safety," The Pew Charitable Trusts, 15 April 2021. https://www.pewtrusts.org/en/research-and-analysis/reports/2020/12/states-can-shorten-probation-and-protect-public-safety

"Statutory Rape." *Wikipedia,* 27 July 2024. https://en.wikipedia.org/wiki/Statutory_rape

"Statutory Rape Between Children Declared Unconstitutional." *Crime & Public Policy.* https://www.koffellaw.com/blog/statutory-rape-between-children-declared-unconst/

Staudt, Sarah. "Winnable Criminal Justice Reforms in 2024." Prison Policy Initiative. November 2023. https://www.prisonpolicy.org/reports/winnable2024.html

Stemen, Don and David Olson. "Looking Deeper at the First Four Months of Illinois' Bail Reform." *Safety+Justice: Challenge,* 18 January 2024. https://safetyandjusticechallenge.org/blog/looking-deeper-at-the-first-four-months-of-illinois-bail-reform/

Stroud, Hernandez D. et al. "A Proposal to Reduce Unnecessary Incarceration." Brennan Center for Justice, 14 March 2023. https://www.brennancenter.org/our-work/policy-solutions/proposal-reduce-unnecessary-incarceration

Swiontkowski, Gale. *Imagining Incest: Sexton, Plath, Rich, and Olds on*

Life with Daddy. Selingrove, PA: Susquehanna University Press, 2003.
Taleb-Karlsson, Akila. "Pleading Guilty: An overview of the French procedure." *Penal Reform International,* 9 January 2017. https://www.penalreform.org/blog/pleading-guilty-overview-french-procedure/#:~:text=Under%20the%20French%20Penal%20Code,may%20not%20exceed%20one%20year.
Taylor, S., Buchanan, J., and Ayres, TC. "Prohibition, Privilege and the Drug Apartheid: The failure of drug policy reform to address the underlying fallacies of drug prohibition." *Criminology and Criminal Justice* 16.4 (2016): 452-469. (1-34). https://researchonline.ljmu.ac.uk/id/eprint/3118/3/Taylor%2C%20Buchanan%20and%20Ayres%20CCJ%20submission%5B1%5D.pdf
Thomas, Wayne H. *Bail Reform in America.* Berkeley: University of California Press, 1976. https://www.google.com/books/edition/Bail_Reform_in_America/60_hEAAAQBAJ?hl=en&gbpv=1&dq=thomas+bail+reform+in+america&pg=PP12&printsec=frontcover
Toda, Saori. "A Place for Public Concerns in Parole Decision Making in Japan." *The Howard Journal of Crime and Justic*e 63.1 (December 25, 2023): 98-117. https://onlinelibrary.wiley.com/doi/full/10.1111/hojo.12550
Tooley, Mark. "Reviving Blue Laws?" *Juicy Ecumenism,* 23 December 2021. https://juicyecumenism.com/2021/12/23/reviving-blue-laws/
Traub, Alex. "Norman Kansfield, 83, Dies; Defrocked for His Daughter's Same-Sex Wedding," *The New York Times* (April 30 [May 2] 2024). https://www.nytimes.com/2024/04/30/us/norman-kansfield-dead.html?searchResultPosition=1
Travers, Max et al. *Rethinking Bail: Court Reform or Business as Usual?* Cha *Switzerland:* Palgrave Macmillan, 2020.
Treen, Barbara Hanson. "Living Slow Deaths Behind Bars." *The New York Times, 3* March 2024. https://www.nytimes.com/2024/03/03/opinion/new-york-parole-reform.html
Tribe, Laurence H. "The Supreme Court's Immunity Decision Is an Outrage." *The New York Times,* 2 July 2024, A18.
Trivedi, Somil. "Coercive Plea Bargaining Has Poisoned the Criminal Justice System. It's Time to Suck the Venom Out." ACLU, 13

January 2020. https://www.aclu.org/news/criminal-law-reform/coercive-plea-bargaining-has-poisoned-the-criminal-justice-system-its-time-to-suck-the-venom-out

Tudosie, Elena Roxana. "Assisted Dying Law Reform: Overcoming the Painful Process that Leads to a Painless Death." PhD thesis. The Open University, 2023. https://oro.open.ac.uk/87047/

Tung, Liz. "After 5-year Battle, New PA Probation Reforms Pushed by Meek Mill Go into Effect." WHYY PBS, 21 June 2024. https://whyy.org/articles/pennsylvania-probation-reforms-act-44-go-into-effect-meek-mill/

Van Brunt, Alexa and Locke E. Bowman. "Toward a Just Model of Pretrial Release: A History of Bail Reform and a Prescription for What's Next." *Journal of Criminal Law and Criminology* 108.4 (Fall 2018): 700-774. https://scholarlycommons.law.northwestern.edu/jclc/vol108/iss4/3

VanSickle, Abbie "Justice Sotomayor Describes Frustration with Being a Liberal on the Supreme Court." *The New York Times,* 24 May 2024. https://www.nytimes.com/2024/05/24/us/politics/sonia-sotomayor-supreme-court.html#:~:text=%E2%80%9CThere%20are%20moments%20when%20I,wipe%20them%20and%20get%20up.%E2%80%9D

VanSickle, Abbie and Michael D. Shear. "Supreme Court, for Now, Blocks Expanded Protections for Transgender Students in Some States." *The New York Times,* 16 August 2024. https://www.nytimes.com/2024/08/16/us/politics/supreme-court-transgender-discrimination-schools.html?searchResultPosition=1

Vermont Ethics Network. "Medical Aid in Dying." 2024. https://vtethicsnetwork.org/palliative-and-end-of-life-care/medical-aid-in-dying-act-39

Viano, Emilio C. "Plea Bargaining in the United States: A Perversion of Justice." *Revue International de Droit Pénal* 83.1.2, 2012. https://www.cairn.info/revue-internationale-de-droit-penal-2012-1-page-109.htm

Waller, Bruce N. *Against Moral Responsibility.* Cambridge: MIT, 2011.

Waller, Bruce N. *Freedom Without Responsibility.* Philadelphia: Temple UP, 1990.

Wegman, Jesse. "There's No Sense of Shame at the Supreme Court." *The New York Times,* 21 May 2024. https://www.nytimes.com/2024/05/21/opinion/supreme-court-alito-flag.html

White, Welsh S. "A Proposal for Reform of the Plea Bargaining Process." *University of Pennsylvania Law Review* 119 (1971): 439-465. https://scholarship.law.upenn.edu/cgi/viewcontent.cgi?article=5815&&context=penn_law_review&&sei-redir=1&referer=https%253A%252F%252Fscholar.google.com%252Fscholar%253Fhl%253Den%2526as_sdt%253D0%25252C46%2526q%253Dplea%252Bbargaining%252Breform%2526btnG%253D#search=%22plea%20bargaining%20reform%22

"Why Probation and Parole." REFORM Alliance 2024. https://reformalliance.com/why-probation-and-parole/

Wice, Paul B. *Freedom for Sale: A National Study of Pretrial* Release. Lexington, MA: Lexington Books, 1974.

Williams, V. L. "Nine Reasons to Go Slow on Bail Bond Reform." *Criminal Justice Review* 3.1, Spring 1978: 9-16. https://www.ojp.gov/ncjrs/virtual-library/abstracts/nine-reasons-go-slow-bail-bond-reform.

Williamson, Jason D. "Antiracist Parole Reform Is Past Due." H*uman Rights Magazine* 48.3 (April 12, 2023). https://www.americanbar.org/groups/crsj/publications/human_rights_magazine_home/economic-issues-in-criminal-justice/antiracist-parole-reform-is-past-due/

Wylie, Stephanie and Ames Grawert. "Challenges to Advancing Bail Reform." Brennan Center for Justice, 10 April 2024. https:/www.brennancenter.org/our-work/research-reports/challenges-advancing-bail-reform

Yang, Crystal S. "Toward an Optimal Bail System." *New York University Law Review* 92 (November 2017): 1399-1493. https://www.nyulawreview.org/wp-content/uploads/2018/08/NYULawReview-92-5-Yang.pdf

Author

Robert Hauptman, a retired university professor, holds a PhD in comparative literature and is a doctoral candidate in library science. He is not a lawyer but briefly studied the law in a formal setting. His ca. 800 publications including 20 books cover a host of topics such as ethics, documentation, authorship, emotions, debunking, mountains, and deserts. He is married to the artist and poet Terry Linda Hauptman, is 83 years old, and has a 24-year-old daughter. He still climbs mountains but probably ascends more slowly than when he was 20.

Made in United States
Orlando, FL
05 November 2026

90230224R00080